THE GONCOURT BROTHERS

By

Richard B. Grant

Edmond and Jules de Goncourt present the fascinating case of two brothers who wrote novels in collaboration. But this unique procedure is not the only reason for writing a book about them, for they had a wide range of interests and abilities. Their work on French art of the eighteenth century is still of value today. They were historians of the French Revolution. They kept a monumental Journal which is a precious document for understanding the world of letters in Paris during the second half of the nineteenth century. As if this were not enough, they painted, did etchings, were influential in introducing Japanese art into France, they experimented with the French language in an attempt to renew it, and in their fiction studied, often with profundity, the interplay of illusion and reality. But perhaps their greatest contribution was to open the world of the novel to the lowest classes of people, and thus to be the initiators of the Naturalistic school of French fiction.

ABOUT THE AUTHOR

Richard B. Grant (b. 1925) took his A.B. and his Ph.D. degrees at Harvard, and taught French language and literature for many years at Duke University. In 1971 he joined the University of Texas at Austin as Professor of French. In addition to collaborating in the writing of two textbooks, he is the author of *Zola's Son Excellence Eugène Rougon: An Historical and Critical Study* and *The Perilous Quest: Image, Myth, and Prophecy in the Narratives of Victor Hugo.* He has also written many articles on French fiction of the nineteenth century.

TWAYNE'S WORLD AUTHORS SERIES

A Survey of the World's Literature

EDMOND AND JULES DE GONCOURT

Portrait by Gavarni, 1853

TWAYNE'S WORLD AUTHORS SERIES (TWAS)

The purpose of TWAS is to survey the major writers—novelists, dramatists, historians, poets, philosophers, and critics—of the nations of the world. Among the national literatures covered are those of Australia, Canada, China, Eastern Europe, France, Germany, Greece, India, Italy, Japan, Latin America, New Zealand, Poland, Russia, Scandinavia, Spain, and the African nations, as well as Hebrew, Yiddish, and Latin Classical literatures. This survey is complemented by Twayne's United States Authors Series and English Authors Series.

The intent of each volume in these series is to present a critical-analytical study of the works of the writer; to include biographical and historical material that may be necessary for understanding, appreciation, and critical appraisal of the writer; and to present all material in clear, concise English —but not to vitiate the scholarly content of the work by doing so.

The Goncourt Brothers

By RICHARD B. GRANT

Duke University

Twayne Publishers, Inc.   ::   New York

Preface

W ITH THE passage of time, the nineteenth century takes on a clearer perspective in contemporary eyes. Figures that had once been considered major, like Pierre Loti and Alphonse Daudet, have faded somewhat. Others have grown steadily in stature, especially Stendhal and Baudelaire, to cite only the most obvious of examples. Caught in the flux of literary popularity are two of the most curious novelists of the century: Edmond and Jules de Goncourt, who had the special distinction of writing in collaboration until Jules's death. Like other nineteenth-century novelists, they were constantly being attacked in the press by representatives of conservatism and "official literature," and they were equally hotly defended by the new, emerging school that we know today as Naturalism. Controversy did not even end when Jules died in 1870, for Edmond continued to write fiction, and was a figure of importance in the world of letters until his death in 1896. But time and the dictates of twentieth-century taste reduced their stature for a while, and although the Académie Goncourt did publish their main works in the 1920's and 1930's, it cannot be denied that there was a general decline in their popularity. Some of this indifference survives today, for the majority of their novels are out of print both in French and in English. But the Goncourts have refused to die that decent literary death of the second-rate novelist, and recent editions of their better novels and the appearance of important critical studies suggest that their worth is beginning to be appreciated once more. The present monograph is not only a tribute to their tenacious survival but also hopes to contribute to the new understanding of their art, to show that they are important writers who should not be neglected.

No effort has been made to present their complete biography, and the many monographs of Edmond and Jules on art history (French and Japanese), political history, the lives of actresses, and the like, receive but cursory attention. Our purpose is to set forth their fictional creation, to show its peculiar nature with its defects and its genius; in short, to assess the value of their novelistic production and to determine their role in the development of the French novel.

RICHARD B. GRANT

The University of Texas at Austin

Contents

Preface

Chronology

1. Into the World of Letters   *13*

2. Early Experiments with the Novel   *33*

3. Exploring the Bourgeoisie and the Working Class   *55*

4. Experiments in the Theater   *73*

5. Their Last Two Novels   *85*

6. Edmond Alone: *La Fille Elisa*   *105*

7. The Brothers Reunited: *Les Frères Zemganno*   *119*

8. *La Faustin* and the Later Years   *131*

9. Conclusion   *143*

    Notes and References   *151*

    Selected Bibliography   *159*

    Index   *161*

Chronology

1822 Edmond de Goncourt born in Nancy, May 26.

1830 Jules de Goncourt born in Paris, December 17.

1834 Death of father, Marc-Pierre Huot de Goncourt.

1847 Edmond takes a minor position in the Treasury.

1848 Death of mother, Annette-Cécile. Edmond serves in the National Guard during the turbulent days of June. Jules passes baccalaureate examination.

1849 Trip by Edmond and Jules to southern France and Algiers. Sketches.

1850 Visit to Switzerland and Belgium. Early attempts at writing for the theater.

1851 Meet Gavarni. Begin keeping their *Journal*. Work for a cousin, Villedeuil, owner of *L'Eclair*. *En 18 . .* published on December 2, the day of the coup d'état.

1852 Contribute to *Le Paris*. Write *La Nuit de Saint-Sylvestre* (play); publish *Le Salon de 1852* (reprints from articles in *L'Eclair*) and *Les Mystéres des Théâtres, 1852*.

1853 *La Lorette* published. Aquitted of charges of licentiousness in the press.

1854 *La Révolution dans les moeurs. Histoire de la Société française pendant la Révolution.*

1855 *Histoire de la Société française pendant le Directoire La Peinture à l'exposition de 1855.* Voyage to Italy.

1856 *Une Voiture de Masques* (reprinted from *Le Paris* and later reissued as *Quelques Créatures de ce temps*). *Les Actrices*.

1856- Meet Théophile Gautier and Gustave Flaubert at the offices
1857 of *L'Artiste*.

1857 *Sophie Arnould* (reworked and republished in 1877). *Portraits intimes du XVIIIe siècle.* Frequent the Moulin Rouge and the Café du Helder with other men of letters.

1858 *Marie Antoinette.*

1859 Jules begins making etchings.

1860 *Les Hommes de Lettres (Charles Demailly). Les Maîtresses de Louis XV.*

1861 *Soeur Philomène.*

1862 *La Femme au XVIIIe siècle.* Death of housekeeper, Rosalie Malingre. Meet Princess Mathilde and George Sand. Magny dinners begin.

1863 Meet Turgenev at Magny dinners.

1864 *Renée Mauperin.*

1865   *Germinie Lacerteux. Henriette Maréchal* produced.

1866   Publication of *Henriette Maréchal. Idées et sensations* (extracts from the *Journal*).

1867   Second Voyage to Italy. *Manette Salomon*.

1868   Buy house in Auteuil. Meet Emile Zola.

1869   *Madame Gervaisais*. Write *Gavarni*.

1870   Death of Jules at Auteuil on June 20. Edmond undergoes siege of Paris.

1873   *Gavarni* published. *La Patrie en danger* published. Meets Alphonse Daudet.

1874-   Meets Guy de Maupassant.
1875

1875   *L'Amour au XVIIIe siècle*

1877   The "Manifeste des Cinq" launched against Zola's *La Terre* by disciples of Edmond. *La Fille Elisa*.

1879   *Les Frères Zemganno*.

1881   *La Maison d'un artiste*.

1882   *La Faustin*. Revelation of plans to establish an Académie Goncourt.

1884   *Chérie*.

1885   Publication of Jules's *Lettres*. Revival of *Henriette Maréchal*. Meets Barbey d'Aurevilly. Inauguration of his "Grenier" or Garret.

1887   *Soeur Philomène* produced as a play at the Théâtre libre. *Renée Mauperin* produced as a play at the Odéon.

1887-   First edition of the *Journal* published in nine volumes.
1896

1888   *Germinie Lacerteux* produced as a play at the Odéon.

1890   Adaptation of *Les Frères Zemganno* and *La Fille Elisa* to the stage.

1891   *Outamaro*.

1892   *Charles Demailly* adapted to the stage.

1893   *La Faustin* adapted for the stage (never produced). *A Bas le progrès* produced (written in 1891).

1896   *Hokousai. Manette Salomon* (adapted for the stage in 1894) produced at the Vaudeville. Death of Edmond on July 16.

1903   First award of prize under the terms of the Académie Goncourt.

1956-   Publication of the entire *Journal*.
1959

CHAPTER 1

Into the World of Letters

I *Childhood and Early Years*

T HE giants of the nineteenth-century novel seemed destined to be creators of fiction from their earliest years. It is true that on occasion one comes across a brilliant amateur like Stendhal who at times preferred heroic action to novelistic creation, or like Fromentin for whom painting was perhaps more important than writing, but others, like Balzac, Flaubert, and Zola revealed early the professional orientation and drive of the true writer. The emergence of the Goncourts into the world of letters was accomplished more slowly. It is necessary to follow this hesitating evolution if we are to understand the preoccupations that led to their becoming creators of fiction.

Descendants of one Antoine Huot, who had purchased the *seigneurie* of Goncourt in Lorraine and who was thus entitled to the aristocratic "de," these noble-born brothers were Parisian to the tips of their fingers, for although Edmond was born in Nancy in 1822, the family moved to the capital shortly thereafter. Their father, Marc-Pierre, was a retired officer of the Napoleonic wars, suffering from ill-health caused by wounds and the arduous campaigns of the Empire. Jules was born in 1830 but could hardly have known his father, who died four years later. His widow received a mere 500-franc pension from the government and therefore experienced some financial difficulties, although she owned farms in Lorraine that provided some revenue. Fortunately, finances permitted the boys to have the usual pattern of schooling. Edmond passed through a certain Pension Goubaux and was then a day pupil at the Collège Bourbon, where in due course Jules followed him. Jules, too, performed acceptably in school, earning prizes in Latin in 1844 and passing the baccalaureate examination brilliantly in 1848. Edmond, who had been studying law since 1841, had for financial reasons abandoned a lawyer's office in order to take a minor

13

position in the Treasury in 1847. He had joined the National Guard
in 1843, and he served actively in the tumultuous days of June, 1848.

But exterior facts and events do not reveal what the young men
were really like. In later years Edmond took pleasure in evoking
their early life. Recalling the summers when the family returned
to Lorraine, he wrote of his father: "I could see him on those sunny
mornings of July and August, striding along so that my little legs
had difficulty in keeping up with him, as he took me with him to
have a glass of water at the *Fountain of Love,* a spring located in
the fields full of daisies."[1] But Marc-Pierre had died when Edmond
was barely an adolescent, and so it is not surprising that the memory
of his father was faint. It was therefore natural that his mother would
leave a far clearer image in his mind. As he stared at a miniature
that he kept by the fireplace, he wrote the following idealized portrait of "a candid face, eyes the color of the sky, a tiny serious mouth
and blond hair." But her beauty had not brought her joy. "Poor
mother," he wrote, "a life full of grief and misfortune." The reference was in part to the father's chronic ill-health, but a personal
recollection came to Edmond's mind as well: "I could see her sweet
sad face, one day when a child, I lay very ill with whooping cough
in her big bed and leaning over me, she had her head near her
brother Armand's . . . after having thrown off the sheet that covered
the corpse-like thinness of my poor little body, she collapsed in
tears in her brother's arms."

The boys survived the hazards of the early years, and when they
reached maturity, they had become handsome young men. All wit-
nesses have agreed about their appearance. Jules was slight of build,
had a long mustache, with fine blond hair that circled his lips. He
often used a monocle. He was apparently very charming. Edmond,
more solidly built, with thick hair, had a short nose and also sported
a mustache. His hands, he claimed, were long and slender, his glance
was cold and piercing but was offset by a sense of native goodness.[2]

Their character and their principal interests were formed early.
In *La Maison d'un artiste,* Edmond evoked the memory of his aunt
Nephtalie de Courmont, who, as André Billy has observed, had a
considerable influence on Edmond and Jules during their formative years.[3] In her Parisian home, she kept a collection of bibelots
and objets d'art, and she succeeded in communicating her sensitivity and taste to the future novelists: "My aunt was at this time
one of four or five people in Paris who had a passion for old things,

for what was deemed beautiful in bygone ages, for Venetian glass, ivory, marquetry furniture, *point d'Alençon* lace and Dresden china." Edmond did indeed love art of this kind, and he also associated with the objects the people who sought or owned them:

In this dim and dusty chaos, there would be luminous women rummaging around, making a pitter-patter like mice in a pile of rubble, and stretching out neatly gloved hands into shadowy corners . . . and daintily drawing back tips of feet shod in *prunella*, then bit by bit thrusting forth into the full light of day pieces of wood-carving or gilded bronze piled up on the ground against the wall . . . and always, at the end of the foray, there would be some lucky find . . . It is those far-off Sundays that have made me the collector of bibelots I have been, and still am, and will remain all my life.[4]

This love of things artistic was becoming visible underneath the rather routine years of education and work in a law office. When still a schoolboy, Jules wrote a drama and equally important, began to sketch. But the direction that their lives were to take was anything but clear when in 1848 their mother died, leaving them alone to make their own decisions. Edmond, now twenty-six years old, took upon himself the role of father of the family, as Jules was still only eighteen.

Money was of course an immediate concern, but in this respect they were forunate. Despite the restrictions that limited income had forced upon them, they did manage to inherit enough of a fortune to be spared the necessity of working for a living. Edmond, who in the misery of his mindless paper-pushing at the Treasury had been contemplating suicide, was now freed from the daily grind. Jules wrote to his friend Louis Passy that the ordinary walks of life were not for him: "I have made a firm resolution and nothing will make me change it, neither sermons, nor good advice . . . *I shall do nothing.*"[5] Years later, Edmond explained what "nothing" really meant: "I had no ambition but that of leading a life of independence in which I could occupy myself with art and literature, but as a dilettante, and not, as it has turned out, a galley-slave of fame."[6] Nothing, in other words, was a life dedicated to art.

The reason for this dedication was not only the result of their natural talents, but a consequence of the historical direction that modern Europe was taking. The Revolution of 1848 showed the depths of popular ferment, not only in France but all over Europe. Edmond served in the National Guard which repressed the popular uprisings in June of that year, and he did so in the belief that the working class should be kept under strict control. He wrote shortly afterward: "Yes, it was necessary to be severe with the ringleaders; yes, it was necessary to be pitiless towards the perpetrators of atrocities that brought dishonor on their party."[7] But he was a realistic conservative, and he judged the reprisals to be excessively severe, if only for practical reasons: "Is it not an established fact that ideas are more formidable when they are watered with the blood of their martyrs?" And then taking a longer view, one that both Edmond and Jules held throughout their lives, the elder saw that "socialist ideas, however absurd they may appear . . . [are] the bases on which a new society, replacing the old, will be established," although to these esthetes, the egalitarian leveling of socialism would be the death of Art as they understood the word. Calling Louis Blanc's doctrine of equality of wages a revolution against talent, Edmond and Jules found the whole social future repugnant and retreated from the political scene. Scorning progress, social utility, and political involvement, Edmond later bragged that he had never voted under the Third Republic. Inevitably, the two brothers were drawn to artists of similar persuasion, to Théophile Gautier who had raised the banner of art for art's sake with the cry "Everything useful is ugly," and to Flaubert who once admired the "wisdom" of a servant who did not even know what kind of government was ruling the country. Art became for the Goncourts, as it became for Flaubert, a religion, and this art was at the antipodes of the *art engagé* of modern figures like Camus and Sartre. In 1860 the Goncourts proclaimed: "Art for Art's sake, art which proves nothing, the music of ideas, the harmony of a sentence, that is our faith and our conscience."[8] They wrote in their *Journal* on April 27, 1862: "The artist, the man of letters, the scholar should never get involved in politics, which is a storm that they ought to let pass beneath them."[9]

II   *Travel and First Efforts at Creativity*

As the previous sentence indicates, the two brothers did not know exactly which was to be their main career, for they had the talent to become—and did become—scholars, artists, and men of letters. Jules's first attempt at drama had dealt with a historical subject (Etienne Marcel), and Edmond, following his baccalaureate, had spent two years in an artist's studio. Faced with the dilemma of the choice of a life's work, they temporized. In 1849, with their financial affairs in order, they decided to hike to southern France. As they went, they sketched and kept a diary, thus combining art and writing. Initially the notes gave merely the usual details of any voyage—the distance traveled, the food eaten, a church sketched. But soon the commentary expanded, and the brothers tried to capture in words what the painter puts on a canvas. The following passage indicates how carefully they worked on their style: "A soot-colored sawmill, with fir sluices, located over a rushing stream, linked to the rock by a bridge against whose wooden pilings the cascade breaks; it rises in stark outline against the bluish silhouette of two rocks, the portals of the Wilderness—Continuous roaring of the torrent, broken by the silvery murmur of a thousand rivulets leaping on all sides."[10]

In this passage, one can observe first the authors' delight in the complex composition of the scene and then their attempt at seizing nuance of color, as one does in a painting. It should also be noted that while the passage is an attempt to make us "see" the reality of the sawmill, it does not try to hide the "artistic" quality of their technique of description, which consciously tries to paint a beautiful picture. The delight in nature is an inheritance from Romanticism, but the techniques emphasize the painter's art and even use synesthesia—before the publication of Baudelaire's *Les Fleurs du mal* —in a phrase like "silvery murmurings" (*susurrement argentin*). These few lines point in the direction of what would become one aspect of their style, the *écriture artiste*, a phrase hard to translate, for "artistic writing" means very little, but which connotes a fine, consciously artistic style of capturing reality without excluding beauty.

Jules and Edmond continued their voyage first to Marseilles and then across the Mediterranean to Algiers. Jules wrote delightedly in November that they had crisscrossed the city with pencil and brush in hand and concluded that there are only two cities in the world: Paris and Algiers. Paris, he explained, is everyone's city; Algiers is the city of the artist. Jules especially was conscious of the riot of color to which he ruefully compared their drab European clothing. But the time spent did not make them neglect their diary in which they tried to capture the sights of the city in verbal form. These notes are, as Fosca remarks, "The first attempts of very gifted amateurs,"[11] and no more than that, but all critics agree that Edmond in his preface to Jules's correspondence summed up well the importance of these notes: "Essentially, this notebook took us away from painting, and made men of letters of us, through the habit that we had little by little developed of putting down in it what we had thought and seen and through our effort which daily became more determined, to find a literary form for our expression."

There is no doubt hindsight to this remark, for when they returned to Paris in December, we find them both doing watercolors at a furious rate. But painting seemed not to satisfy them long, and they resumed their travels, visiting first Switzerland and Belgium and then the Norman coast. During this trip they tried their hand at literature, for Jules wrote in Normandy nineteen chapters of what was to be their first "novel," *En 18 . . .* However, still uncertain of the course they wished to take, when they returned to Paris in 1850 they tried their hand at writing for the theater. The first two skits, whose manuscripts have been lost and which were never published, were vaudevilles refused at the Palais-Royal entitled *Sans Titre* and *Abou Hassan*. There followed *La Nuit de Saint-Sylvestre* in 1852. It was refused by the Comédie Française. These can hardly be considered major efforts.

III   En 18. .

The distinction of being their true *coup d'essai* goes to the above-mentioned *En 18 . .* , published on December 2, 1851. The story of its appearance has been amusingly told by Edmond in a preface to the 1884 Brussels edition:

On December 1, 1851, we went to bed in the beatific frame of mind of young authors awaiting the appearance of their first volume, dreaming of innumerable editions, when cousin Blamont . . . came noisily into my room:
— By God, it's happened!
— What's happened?
— The *coup d'état.*
— Oh no! our novel was to go on sale today!
— Your novel . . . any novel . . . France couldn't care less about novels today.

The distressing news was only too true. Even the advertising for the volume was nowhere in evidence. According to Edmond's account, the editor Gerdès had burned the publicity sheets fearing that the cabalistic title might evoke Napoleonic memories of the eighteenth of Brumaire. *En 18 . .* sold very poorly indeed, but the Goncourts did have one stroke of luck. The influential critic Jules Janin gave it a lengthy review in the *Journal des Débats*, no doubt because Jules de Goncourt's style directly imitated that of Janin. However, nothing could make this work popular, and politics were hardly to blame. The book is difficult, at times almost incomprehensible, and has repelled most readers and critics. It is usually dismissed as a youthful oddity. Even Edmond himself was harsh on their trial effort, calling it in that same preface an "interesting embryo of our later novels, a first book containing in a very curious way the beginning of the virtues and defects of our talent." He stated frankly that he thought the book a poor one, explaining that "It has an annoying striving for wit, dialogue made with sentences out of a book, a flirtation of unbelievable falseness. As for the style, it is still inlaid too much with the first Romanticism of 1830, with its tinsellike phoniness. We made natural comparisons of the skin of women with *amalgoliths*, and blueish tints of black hair with tempered coulauxa steel." This weakness, Edmond went on to say, was the result of their not yet having a "direct vision of humanity. It had its source in books." He did claim in its behalf, however, that it revealed what would be the future direction of French letters: determinism, pessimism, and the taste for Japanese art. We stated above that most critics have dismissed the book as a youthful oddity. After Janin's review which in its own bravura tone recaptures the style of *En 18 . .* but hardly deals with the text, we find that praise is lacking even in Delzant's semiofficial biography. He calls the work "bizarre and cabalistic."[12] More recently Fosca has concluded: "Under the sparkling cover, there is nothing or almost nothing."[13] In general, critics have been content to repeat Edmond's own analysis.

The only serious attempt to grapple with this unsung but in fact important piece of fiction has been made by Robert Ricatte, who argues that *En 18 . .* is not obscure and inchoate, and that the apparently formlessness is a bit of deception practiced by the authors.[14] For Ricatte, the text is basically a novel in the manner of Balzac, if one can see through the *trompe l'oeil* of the surface. One chapter, entitled "Sketch of the Nineteenth Century," offers the true title, he claims; and with a base of contemporary sociology, we have the makings of a novel. Further, although the disgressions and the absence of transitions make the next almost an enigma, there is a co-

herent plot: The hero, an artist names Charles, is in love with two
women, a Jewish model and a German aristocrat. The outcome is
that Charles is disillusioned by both women (the German turns out
to be a spy) and commits a form of suicide by retreating from the
world, abandoning art, and becoming an antiquarian. The analysis
of women and their destructive effect on men suggests to Ricatte a
parallel with Balzac, whose "studies of women" often had the
theme of the destruction of man, as is evident by such works as
La Duchesse de Langeais and *La Cousine Bette*. Viewing *En 18 . .*
as a Balzacian novel leads Ricatte to conclude that it is a very poor
novel. Their hero is superficially characterized and quite unreal,
and he is even contradictory. On the one hand, he is without social
ambition; on the other he is lured by the German woman into striving for "success" in society. On the one hand, he is a cool detached
cynic; on the other, he is a person who can be destroyed by love.
Ricatte concludes that nothing in these "temptresses" permits us
to imagine the disastrous effect they will have on Charles's latent
genius.[15]

It is a mistake, however, to view *En 18 . .* as a traditional novel
in disguise, for the novelistic elements are so feeble and so submerged
that they almost do not exist. In point of fact, the Goncourts were
experimenting with new departures in fiction and were reacting
against the "typical" novel. Throughout their lives they rejected
plot as an organizing principle of fiction, even when they found
themselves obliged—by the very traditions of the fiction of their
age—to use one. What is at work here is an attempt to organize fiction not along the usual lines of linear plot, but thematically.
Edmond in the preface quoted above, saw the themes as those of
determinism and pessimism. But these are themes generated by a
yet deeper vision, the central theme of doubt, which in its turn is
a creation of the phenomenon of illusion in human existence. It is
no accident that the first chapter—entitled significantly "The Last
Word"—apostrophizes life in this manner: "Life!—O men, my colleagues, my brothers, fallen like me on this bit of dried mud, without
a map, without a passport, launched like me as children lost on that
vague highway of humanity between *Who knows?* and *Maybe,* show
me the executioner's wall" (25). The text goes on to pronounce
that mankind's traditional answers to the enigma of existence, the
Church's call to prayer, the senses' call to enjoyment, ambition's
call to action—all these are lies. The subsequent chapters will doc-

ument in detail this gloomy view of man's condition.

First, we enter the artist's studio and without any description or preparation are greeted by pages of dialogue full of youthful paradoxes, whose function is to make a clean sweep of conventional morality. Typical quotes are: "A sunny day, a pipe, and a big woman who has all the moral qualities of a pillow, that is my recipe for paradise" (32); "marriage is Dante's inferno with a Daumier frontispiece" (39); and so it goes through religion, royalty, the empire and all politics (45). Some of the dialogue is so odd it seems as if the Goncourts are trying to mock conventional fiction with its normal development and to create a curiously modern literature of the absurd:

"—I've always had the idea of cross-breeding animals."

"—Sure, you would have deported Hoffman to the Isle of Patmos, so that he could bring back sketches of beasts."

"—Why not cross elephants and camels?"

"—Why not ants and sour herrings?"

It all fits the theme of *Who Knows?* and *Maybe.*

At the end of this chapter, the hero is introduced. He wakes up in a corner of the atelier and hears someone mention originality. Whereupon Chapter II delivers a four-page monologue showing that there is nothing new under the sun, and it fits in neatly with a pessimistic view of life that sees this reality under the illusions of novelty or progress. The hero, sad and cynical, has been taught by prostitutes that there is no tomorrow. He is indifferent to politics and is interested only in art. We next see him at the theater where he spies the Jewess for the first time. The emphasis of this chapter is not on a budding love affair but on the mime on stage who is acting out the disintegration of personality under intoxication, as if to say that under our pleasant exteriors future decay is to be found. At the end of the performance, we are treated to a final irony. Next to the beautiful girl is seated an ancient crone peeling an orange: beauty becomes age; all is vanity. This has little to do with plot development but much to do with pessimism and illusion. Under beauty, age is lurking; behind the actor's mask lies the truth of our sorry estate.

This interlude is followed by the meeting of Charles and Hertha von Riedmassen, the German spy. The young woman, described by a mutual friend as "one of those beautiful dreams that you dream one evening," underscores the theme of illusory appearance once more, for Charles does not yet know her maleficent nature. Their conversations and letters are cynical in tone, and she writes to him of her disillusion in love and her discovery of "sad reality," no longer believing in those resurrections of virginity through love (209)so dear to the Romantics. In an essay chapter that deals directly with the absurdity of life, we read: "Human will, free will, big heady words that intoxicate our pygmy natures that whirl under the enigmatic flagellation of fate" and "an animal born by chance, developing by chance, dying by chance, comes, goes, twists and turns, stops, weakens and falls there where it is written: Here lies." The final statement is a categorical: "Down with illusion" (111-14). Even objects figure in this symphony of cynicism, illusion and doubt. One chapter is dedicated to the rococco interior of the Ried-massen house, with the emphasis on the twisted, tortuous forms of statuary and bibelots of which the Goncourts were so fond. Words like "capricious," "rolled," "swarming," "mosaic," "intertwining," and "convulsive" all suggest the breakdown of the classical ideal of clarity. As a final irony, the list of objects ends with the mold of a medal showing a head of Ernest the Pious on a decoration celebra-ting the renewal of the ancient order of German probity. As the Goncourts were chauvinistic in the extreme and as the Von Ried-massens are revealed as spies, we realize the bitterness of the authors' irony.

And so it continues. Paris is evoked as a place where money makes a name, love is defined through cheating, and people are ruined by trying to appear grandiose (139). Even the idyll in the forest with the Jewess is a bitter joke, for just as it is progressing nicely, the hard voice of the girl's mother shatters the illusion, and he is left alone. After many a cynical page, we glimpse a brief vision of Art as the only true thing in life, but even it cannot compensate for the horror of human existence. Destroyed by Woman's duplicity, Charles begins dreaming that he is being guillotined while he hears the mocking laughter of a woman in the background. Significantly, the chapter is entitled "Through the Gates of Horn," thus making clear from the Homeric quote that what the hero had thought was the world of ideal dream, Homer's Gates of Ivory, must yield to the reality of the Gates of Horn.

Thus, *En 18 . .* has considerable coherence of composition pro-vided that we do not try to view it as a novel. But what can we call it? Jules, in a letter to Louis Passy in June, 1859, spoke admiringly of Byron's *Don Juan*, describing it in language that fits *En 18 . .* neatly:

"It has, or rather insists on, every digression, any number of theatrical asides. All you have to do is to dress it up in rhyme and all the ideas that go through your head, and for lovers of winged fantasy, this is a priceless liberty."[16] In 1851 when feeling unappreciated, Jules likened their own work to that of Sterne. The juxtaposition is an excellent one. *Tristram Shandy* (1760-67) of Laurence Sterne has the same "incoherent" structure to judge by novelistic standards, the same love of wit and digression, the same primacy given to ideas. *En 18 . .* twice refers to Sterne's work (99, 105) and even asks openly: "Is this a novel [*roman*] a novella [*nouvelle*], a study [*étude*]? Who knows?" (149).

To answer this question of a "formless" work of fiction that takes on form when one focuses on theme and idea, it is of value to consider this text as an example of a separate genre of fiction, one that Northrop Frye has called the anatomy.[17] Frye defines it as "not primarily concerned with the exploits of heroes" but as that which relies on the free play of intellectual fancy and on the kind of humorous observation that produces caricature. Further, "the intellectual structure built up from the story makes for violent dislocations in the customary logic of narrative."[18] In this kind of writing, characterization seems to be "stylized rather than naturalistic, and presents people as mouthpieces of the ideas they represent,"[19] and in *En 18 . .* it is true that the characters are stylized to some extent, being subordinated to the thematic and intellectual thrust of the work. In summary, *En 18 . .* is a piece of fiction that presents a systematically pessimistic view of the nineteenth century. It claims that all morality, all idealisms are illusions. Secular humanism and the doctrine of progress are repudiated; society is labeled as false, politics as vanity; the family is meaningless; love, women, and marriage are a horrible trap; and man is weak before this grim world where people and objects appear good but are in reality evil. We have, then, in this trial effort of Jules and Edmond a fascinating, rather brief anatomy or dissection of their times, a work that should only secondarily be considered in the novelistic tradition. It has been unjustly neglected.

This fiction, even by the standards that we have set forth above, has a weakness, one that points to the unique feature of the two brothers' creative effort, namely their collaboration. In *En 18 . .* the technique was simple: Jules wrote some chapters, and Edmond wrote the others. At this time their styles were markedly different, and the difference is quite visible. Edmond wrote in the heavy descriptive style of Théophile Gautier, whereas Jules's style was sprightly, paradoxical, a perpetual display of fireworks. The two did not fit very well. But with practice, the brothers learned to write in closer harmony. Delzant summarized their methods as follows:

> When it came to writing a book, the two brothers, in the inspiration of tobacco smoke, arranged the outline, combined, agreed on this or that bit of description that they remembered having put in their notebooks, all this taking some time. The subject to be treated soon split in their minds into a certain number of distinct tableaux, the work was born with its various limbs, its beginning and its end. They started at the two ends first, because they were the more important. Each one retired to a room and wrote the same chapter. When they read it aloud, they chose the better one.[20]

As Ricatte observes, they didn't quite choose the "better one" that simply, for in fact they often used part of one effort to enrich the other.[21] As for the intervening chapters, "the rest of the book was composed according to the whim of inspiration [*au hasard de l'inspiration*], without preconceived order, until all the threads covered the plot, until it was time to make a definite revision."[22] As for the revisions, the brothers, especially Jules, labored like slaves to find just the right adjective or epithet. This technique of composition indicates why the novels lack a linear plot line and why the Goncourts' instincts led them in the direction of separate individual chapters organized around a theme. But the difficulty was that such fiction was not popular, would not sell; and thoroughly discouraged, they abandoned fiction for nearly a decade.

IV   *The Goncourts and the World of Journalism*

In the nineteenth century, journalism offered a common way of working into the world of letters, for poetry often appeared in periodicals like *L'Artiste*, and prose fiction was habitually serialized. By chance, a cousin of the Goncourts, the Comte de Villedeuil, decided in 1851 to found a literary periodical (a weekly review of literature and the arts). He offered the two brothers important posts as editors, and in January, 1852, *L'Eclair* appeared for the first time. Villedeuil's financial position was precarious and *L'Eclair* was already in distress when he founded another weekly, *Le Paris*, intended for a broader audience. Through these papers the Goncourts became intimately acquainted with journalists and also found an outlet for their own efforts. Gavarni, Nadar, Murger, and Théodore de Banville were the best known of those who worked on these periodicals, but there were many others, mostly of Bohemian mores, whom in later years the more successful Goncourts were to abandon entirely.

The brothers' literary contributions to these newspapers were of three kinds. Their first play, a fantasy called *La Nuit de Saint-Sylvestre*, was published in *Le Paris* in 1852. Perhaps more significant was a series of sketches of real personalities, sometimes slightly disguised, and various vignettes of Parisian life. They collected these articles under the title *Une Voiture de masques* (1856).[23] These sketches foreshadow the brothers' later attempts to describe a person or a scene in a few brief paragraphs. The third aspect to their work was art criticism. Reprints from *L'Eclair* were put together to form a volume, *Le Salon de 1852*; and another volume, which also appeared in 1852, offered a collection of theatrical reviews. It was entitled *Les Mystères des Théâtres*

The experience of working in journalism led to an incident that had a marked effect upon them. They arose one morning in 1852 to discover that they were being arrested for having committed "an outrage against public morality." The offending article was merely the account of a whimsical stroll through Paris which commented on the passing scene (again the tendency toward "anatomy"). In so doing, they had quoted a few mildly erotic verses from the Renaissance poet Jacques Tahureau, which had already been printed in Sainte-Beuve's *Tableau de la Poésie au XVIe siecle*. They rushed around to visit the judges (a common custom in those days) and discovered to their horror that the assistant prosecuting attorney believed in their innocence but would prosecute them fully because he had his orders. So much for "justice," concluded the Goncourts. It was another example of a comforting illusion being torn away by ugly reality. They were acquitted on February 19, 1853, but they were not mollified. That they, dedicated only to Art, could be so pilloried was a shock that they would not soon forget. They branded the regime as barbarous and corrupt. They saw hypocrisy everywhere. The experience also eased them out of the world of journalism and into the safer life of historians of the past.

V   *The Goncourts as Art Critics*

Their love for painting, etching, and bibelots made them historians and critics of eighteenth-century art. Between 1859 and 1870 they composed a dozen monographs on painters of the preceding century and had Dentu publish them at their own expense. These were: *Les Saint-Aubin* (1859), *Watteau* (1860), *Prud'hon* (1861), *Boucher* (1862), *Greuze* (1863), *Chardin* (1864), *Fragonard* (1865), *Debucourt* (1866), *La Tour* (1867), and *Les Vignettistes Gravelot, Cochin-Eisen, Moreau*, in two parts from 1868 to 1870. These individual studies were put together and published in 1875 under the title *L'Art du dix-huitième siècle*.

As lovers of the past, they were horrified that the great works of the eighteenth century were being neglected, and they attacked with feeling the prejudice that reigned during the early part of the nineteenth century. No doubt because of the widespread feeling against the *ancien régime*, the works of masters (major and minor) were going for a song in the displays of second-hand dealers, growing moldy on walls, or disappearing into foreign collections. Even Watteau's famous *Embarquement pour Cythère* was unappreciated: "Do you know where it is buried, hidden, cast away? In a studio of the Academy, where it serves as a target for the laughter and the spitballs of David's art students."[24]

Thus one of their principal purposes in doing art history was to remind France that a glorious heritage was being neglected. The Goncourts, themselves artists, spoke accurately and shrewdly at times about technique. For instance, they could observe how in a still life the dominant color tones were carried over with great subtlety from one center of interest to another. They could also comment on the sociological implications of an artist, considering Chardin, for example, the epitome of the bourgeoisie and the spokesman for his class. But the main desire of Jules and Edmond was less to interpret the past than to bring it to life. Operating on the reasonable assumption that the art of the previous century was almost unknown, they tried to transpose into words what was visible on canvas, to capture the tone as well as the image. Here, for instance is part of their evocation of the *Embarquement pour Cythère*:

Love is the light of this world. It penetrates it and fills it. It is its youth and its serenity; and passing through the rivers and mountains, promenades and gardens, the lakes and fountains, Watteau's paradise open up: It is Cythera. Under a sky painted in summer colors, Cleopatra's galley hesitates by the shore. The water is still. The woods are silent. From the lawn to the firmament, beating the still air with their butterfly wings, a swarm of Cupids flies, flies, plays and dances, uniting with roses nonchalant couples, forming a chain above the whirl of kisses rising from earth to heaven. . . .[25]

There is no denying the charm of these evocations which, coupled with the serious study and technical competence of the two brothers, earned for them a genuine place in the history of art criticism. Their only weaknesses were, in André Billy's opinion, "narrowness of taste" and the need for "greater historical perspective of the evolution of art" (72). The judgment is sound.

This excursion into art criticism was not without its effect on their development as future novelists. In describing these unknown masterpieces of the past so that they could come alive through words, the brothers were in fact reinforcing tendencies already visible in their descriptive prose technique, as we saw from their travel diary. Hence in their fiction, details of a room, a person, and so on, almost seem to be descriptions of a painting. There is often a heavy emphasis on light and shadow, on detail of color, and on composition, and there are even explicit parallels to the styles of various painters. But the technique transposed to prose fiction is double-edged. It if captures nuance, it loses power and directness. Frequently a Goncourt descriptive seems to be made at one remove, becoming a description of a picture of a landscape, a room, or a person.

VI   *The Goncourts as Historians*

Their other manner of exploring the past was as social historians. In 1854, the Goncourts published their *L'Histoire de la société française pendant la Révolution*. They were to write in 1862 concerning their own *La Femme au XVIIIe siècle*: "a century is near us. It gave birth to our own. . . . It is a human era, it is the French century *par excellence*." They go on to claim: "This century, strangely enough has hitherto been neglected by History. Historians have pushed it aside as too compromising for their dignity. . . . Neglected by History, the eighteenth century became the prey of the novel and the theater . . . and it was finally made a legendary century of comic opera." Here, the preoccupation to find the truth beneath the layers of illusion makes itself insistent: "We wish, if possible, to find once again and to tell the truth about this unknown or badly known century."[26] Was the preceding century really so unknown? Probably not, as far as "official" political history was concerned,[27] but the Goncourts had a different vision. As they wrote in the preface to *Les Maîtresses de Louis XV*: "It will no longer be only the official acts of nations [*peuples*], the public and exterior acts of a state or a social system, wars, combats, peace treaties. . . . Social history will be that disdained by political history."

To achieve this end, they realized that they must have personal documents as well as official ones. Their instincts drew them to private correspondence, memoirs, novels, brochures, and newspapers. Their theory was matched by their practice. They bought old letters and used them. Curcio, studying their initial effort, does not hesitate to conclude that the number of sources employed was impressive, but even so there were weaknesses in their method. The Goncourts' disdain for progress and for the masses was reflected in their horror of the French Revolution. Because of this bias they neglected revolutionary newspapers, choosing other material that fit their thesis.[28] Further, they treated all documentation as equally valuable, unwilling to see that their own favorite sources could be heavily biased.

The following year (1855) saw the publication of a companion work, *L'Histoire de la Société française pendant le Directoire*, which was savagely attacked by the influential economist Henri Baudillart in the *Débats*. André Billy surmises, probably correctly, that this negative reception may well have discouraged the Goncourts from continuing as official historians of a period, for they had once projected a history of France during the Empire.[29] Instead they turned to biography, a genre they cultivated with some success, for it involved less complete coverage of an era. A biography of the singer Sophie Arnould appeared in 1857 (Edmond revised and improved it in 1877), and also in that year *Portraits intimes du XVIIIe siècle* appeared. Perhaps their major effort in this line was their biography of Marie Antoinette, published in 1858, although like some of their other works of history and biography it was considerably expanded and revised for a second edition (1859). The author's announced purpose was again to see beyond the stereotypes or the mask that legend has grafted onto the person, to discover—by means of personal documents—the individual as she really was, to set her properly in an historical landscape. Other monographs were *Les Maîtresses de Louis XV* (1860),[30] followed by the more generalized essay *La Femme au XVIIIe siècle* in 1862. Edmond judged some of this work harshly, as when he wrote in 1878 in a revised preface to *Les Maîtresses de Louis XV*: "The book has too much pretty rhetoric, too many bits of literature, too much bravura placed side by side, without a narrative that stretches them out and links them together." He also claimed that the sense of the passage of time was weak and categorized the work as too summary and too hastily written.[31]

Despite the above self-criticism, the Goncourts felt that they had made a modest contribution to the development of historiography. As Edmond put it in 1878: "I have the feeling that in history there will soon emerge from beneath the earth a generation . . . that will write history in imitation of my manner."[32] Even so, they were not destined to exploit this historical vein much more. By 1862 one can sense a weariness with the subject in that they find ancient (classical) history and art too impersonal to engage their interest. While never repudiating their early efforts, they state in 1865: "Certainly we galvanized history, as much as is possible, and galvanized it with truth truer than that of others. . . . Well, this truth which is dead no longer says anything to us."[33] Their interest in things modern was becoming stronger. Although they disliked contemporary society in many ways, they were to become its chroniclers. Their *Journal; Mémoires de la vie littéraire* is a major document of nineteenth century history in its literary, social and even political aspects. It was begun on that day in December, 1851, that *En 18 . .* was published.

VII *The Journal*

The *Journal*, as it is normally called, was, according to Delzant (who obtained the information from Edmond), composed as follows: "Ever since their début in the world of letters, the Goncourts rather regularly kept note of all the things which struck them and the events which took place before their eyes. Each evening, in one of those notebooks made for school-children, one of the brothers, but more often Jules, began to write while the other, behind him, suggested a picturesque touch, enlived a word with an epithet or reinforced an expression."[34] Edmond emphasized the collaboration involved: "The *Journal* is our confession of each evening . . . of two lives, inseparable in pleasure, work and grief,"[35] although he insisted that the entire manuscript was written by Jules but under dicatation by both of them. After Jules's death, Edmond continued to keep the

diary and in 1887 published the first volume of an expurgated
version. Despite omissions intended to keep the author from having
a lawsuit on his hands, the volumes were greeted with hostility, for
the brothers had frequently been more than frank—even scurrilous
—in their revelations. Even the Daudets, Edmond's closest friends,
breathed a sigh of relief when the publications came to an end with
the ninth volume in 1896. The unexpurgated version was not to
appear until 1956-59, edited by Robert Ricatte.

What is the *Journal*? Can it be viewed as more than just a mine of
information? Can we treat it as a work of art in itself? Kenneth Rexroth, for one, believed so. In his "Classics Revisited" column in the
Saturday Review (October 22, 1966), he attributed to it the labels of
"drama" and of "epic"—two words that surely imply literary form.
He further saw in the *Journal* not a "random diary" but a coherent
intellectual construct which made its authors the Gibbon, if not the
Toynbee, of their age: "We can watch little tarts work their way up
the ladder of important men until they are completely accepted
socially. Against them is counterpointed a contrary movement—
writers and generals and ministers age, lose control, decline and
fall." The *Journal* is indeed a fascinating document, and its importance is underlined by the fact that it has been frequently translated,
in whole or in part.[36] But it does not truly have the contrapuntal
structure that Rexroth claims for it. The patterns of rise and fall
seem really to take place at random, and the system of daily jottings
often kept the material from being more artistically organized by the
authors' imaginative processes. It remains a precious document of
the age, but no more.

Thus the Goncourts' concern with history extended both into the
past, with their histories, biographies, and art criticism, and into the
present with their *Journal*. As they came to realize that their primary
interest was in the present, they attributed their vocation as novelists
to their work as historians: "Our literary path is rather odd. We
passed through history to arrive at the novel. This is hardly the usual
pattern. And yet, we acted very logically. On what basis does one
write history? On the basis of documents. And the documents of the
novel [*roman*] are life." Here we are faced with the problem of the
meaning of the word *roman*, which is used in French to cover about
all forms of prose fiction. As fiction, the Goncourts did not like the
roman, for it conjured up eighteenth-century adventure tales and
more generally the "untruths" of romance. Since Balzac, they

argued, the novel no longer has the meaning that older generations gave to the word. The modern novel must be made with documents taken from nature, just as history is made from written documents.[37] As a result, "one of the most particular characteristics of our novels will be to be the most historical ones of this era, to be those which will furnish the largest number of *facts* and *truths* concerning the social history of this century."[38] A few months later, they created an even tighter bond between fiction and history with their famous quote: "History is a novel that has existed; the novel is history that might have existed."[39] More than history is involved in these quotations. The insistence on truth versus falsehood is obvious and will—in the form of illusion and reality—take on new life in the novels of the 1860's when the Goncourts were to deal with social problems.

CHAPTER 2

Early Experiments with the Novel

I Charles Demailly

THE idea for their next work of fiction first blossomed during the 1850's when the Goncourts frequented the Café Riche and became acquainted with men of letters, both noble and ignoble. In the summer of 1858 they were hard at work, and the manuscript was finished by 1859. Unable to arrange its serialization in the press, they had it published in book form directly, by Dentu in January, 1860, under the title *Les Hommes de lettres*. It was not until the second edition (1868) that the title was changed to *Charles Demailly*, by which name it is known today. Commenting in 1895 on the composition of the novel, Edmond wrote that it had been written more by Jules than by himself, as one could sense by the presence of many chapters full of fanciful dialogue, whereas he, Edmond, had worked on the "architecture" of the novel.[1] One can gather from this remark that the fusion of style that the two brothers had been seeking was still anything but achieved by 1859 and was a reason why the novel was—and still is—greeted with something less than enthusiasm.

Another reason for critical hostility was the subject matter, as a plot summary will make clear. The hero, Charles Demailly, writes for a nasty little newspaper called *Le Scandale*. Wrenching himself free from the harmful influence of his cronies on the newspaper staff, he regains some sense of personal mission, isolates himself, and writes a serious novel of high quality. Because of his integrity, his former "friends" attack him mercilessly in the columns of the paper and in the cafés. At this juncture he marries an actress, Marthe, and after an idyllic honeymoon he discovers that she is heartless and stupid. Little by little she destroys him, with the help of a former colleague on the *Scandale* who is jealous of his true success. Marthe gives this man some letters written by her husband who, when in a whimsical mood, had caricatured some of his best friends. This final betrayal causes the hero's madness, and he is eventually locked up in an asylum as a hopeless idiot.

It is clear from this summary that the world of journalism receives harsh treatment in *Charles Demailly*, and journalist-critics were quick to seek revenge. Jules Janin, who had liked *En 18 . .* , now accused the brothers of creating "a scurrilous diatribe against their own kind, a tableau which leads one to scorn the world of letters."[2] Only George Sand, living in retirement in the country, wrote them an encouraging letter. She admired their eloquent satire, although even she was shocked at the venality of this Parisian world of letters that they had created in their fiction. But it was not only the victims of the satire who have found the novel wanting. Delzant's only interest in it centers on biographical elements that can be culled from it. Fosca is very harsh, complaining of too many speeches, ridiculous scenes, a general preachiness, and bad organization,[3] and André Billy calls it full of disorder and confusion and accords it only historical interest.[4] Clearly a new look at the text needs to be made if we are to deal with it at all.

En 18 . . opened in an artist's studio, but as we observed in the previous chapter, we do not see the locale, which is submerged under a flood of repartee. In *Charles Demailly* the milieu is described in detail; we see the directors of *Le Scandale* in their offices where they are presented clearly, one by one (although too mechanically), in the normal tradition of the novel. The characters involved are closely copied from real life. In the *Journal* entry for March 31, 1861, the brothers gave the key. Under the thin fictional disguise are visible acquaintances of the Goncourts: Monselet, Scholl, Nadar, Venet, Claudin, Valentin, Villemessant, and Gaïffe, names known today only to the specialist, but who at the time were fairly prominent figures. Each of these personages reveals his character through jokes, puns, and plans for scurrilous articles. For example, the editor Montbaillard (Villemessant) examines the proofs for the next issue and exclaims: "A lousy issue—It doesn't say a thing, it doesn't nail anyone. All the people it mentions will have a comfortable night!" This theme of venal journalism was a frequent one in the nineteenth-century fiction, the best known examples no doubt being Balzac's *Illusions Perdues* (1837-43) and Maupassant's *Bel-Ami* (1885), and this interest reflected the depths to which the fourth estate had fallen. *Charles Demailly* also links the nasty little group of *Le Scandale* to the specific society of their times. These journalists even develop certain characteristics of their occupation. "A life of struggles, the never-ending pin-pricks and sufferings that his self-esteem had to endure, the constant defeats or at least the disappointments that wounded his pride . . . maintain the man of letters in a state of acrimony. . . . Armed by intimate daily suffering which toughens his hide, he loses his sensitivity, tenderness, delicacy and also gratitude" (110).

When evening falls, the offices are vacated and life continues in the cafés. Here the Goncourts made use of their own experience. It had been their custom to gather after the theater at midnight at the Café Riche with Mario Uchard, Paul de Saint-Victor, Henri Murger, the former Bohemian, and others. As the brothers noted in the *Journal*, the Café Riche was becoming the camp of writers of elegance where, because of all the gold, the white and red carpet, none of the scum dared enter.[5] But despite the elite clientele the conversation was anything but exalted, at times merely filthy without being even witty. Thus in reality elegance and inelegance were mingled; when the Goncourts later transferred the café scenes to fiction, they eliminated the elegance. The meetings in the novel feature the cynical journalists of *Le Scandale* but carefully omit writers of quality, so that when Charles abandons his Bohemian cronies for a higher literary sphere, the contrast is more startling. In this change, too, the Goncourts chronicled their own emancipation from Bohemianism to a more elite group.

Charles' new circle of friends is again a transposition of reality. The man who makes this higher vision possible, Boisroger, is a copy of the poet Théodore de Banville. The new group gathers at the Moulin Rouge (a place well known to Edmond and Jules) and includes fictionalized versions of Théophile Gautier and Gustave Flaubert, both of whom the Goncourts had met at the periodical *L'Artiste* during the winter of 1856-57. Ricatte also suspects the presence of Barbey d'Aurevilly under the character Franchemont. These figures were giants of their day; the conversation that the Goncourts ascribe to their fictional counterparts fittingly treats both literature and ideas with dedicated seriousness. There is a genuineness and authenticity here whose function is to show up the shoddiness of the first group of Bohemians.

The plot finally begins when Charles meets Marthe. Again, reality provided the details of what seems to be a facile piece of fiction. Their friend Mario Urchard confessed to them in August, 1858, that his actress-wife, Madeleine Brohan, became bored and trans-

ported her stage roles as villainess into their *ménage*, needled her
husband with calculated subtlety, and even tried by lying to dishonor him in the eyes of his friends. Her hardness of heart was unbelievable. One day, when in exasperated fury Uchard butted his
head against the wall in an effort to dash out his brains, Madeleine
commented laconically: "You sure are a failure!" ("Tu t'es raté").[6]
The Goncourts kept the details of this personal tragedy and made it
the backbone of the narrative structure of their fictional text.[7]

Because the development of the fiction is so heavily sociological
throughout all the chapters that examine the world of letters, and
because Marthe's evil nature is not revealed for some time, the
novel unfolds at a very slow pace during the first part, only to explode violently as the denouement approaches. Ricatte finds a
close parallel with Balzac's technique, just as he did with *En 18* . . .
In the case of *Charles Demailly*, Ricatte's comparison seems reasonably appropriate. Balzac does at times have a slow preparation for
a violent resolution. Marthe's betrayal of her husband with
Nachette's help, at the same time that Couturat is trying to acquire
the newspaper and to eliminate Nachette, does indeed fit the
exciting and melodramatic tradition of *Le Père Goriot* and *La
Cousine Bette*. The story is structured around four basic parts: (1) the
sociology of the world of letters, (2) the love of Charles for Marthe,
(3) the plot crisis, and (4) Charles's final disintegration. Ricatte
sees value in each of the parts, but his main reservation concerns
the manner in which they come together. He calls the whole things
"hybrid," claiming that the text oscillates between realism and
fantasy and that sometimes detailed "Balzacian" descriptions
appear where there is no need for them. He also makes clear his
belief that the Goncourts are too harsh on women and that the final
"medical" diagnosis is not entirely sound. In short, Ricatte aligns
himself with the traditional view of *Charles Demailly*, which sees
the novel at best as a preparation for the later works.[8]

It may seem odd to dwell at such length on one of the Goncourts'
"lesser" works, but an entire esthetic concept is at stake. Ricatte
himself observes that *Charles Demailly* is something of a reprise of
En 18 . ., that it treats a similar hero, whose destruction is achieved
at the hands of women, and that it explores the world of letters as
their first fictional effort dealt with the world of art. Both include set descriptive pieces of nature, and as far as style is concerned, both lack smooth chapter transitions, although this is less

true of *Charles Demailly*. Perhaps the most fruitful manner of comparing the two would be to suggest that while their earliest effort subordinated narrative plot to thematic "anatomy," in *Charles* the two are given about equal importance. The quality of anatomy is still very strong in this latter work, so strong that the Goncourts humorously parodied the critics of their fiction within the body of the novel. When Charles's cronies of the Café Riche dissect his fine novel, one exclaims: "No plot!" The text conveys the scorn of the journalist but also the author's scorn at this facile judgment. Edmond later sneered at Zola who was trying to find some action for *La Joie de vivre*, saying "he needs action because he is no analyst,"[9] and in 1886 he bragged of his own novels "without adventures, but always with interesting characters."[10] He rejoiced in that same year to be "rid of the idiotic complications of plot composition."[11] The result of downgrading plot is, of course, to reinforce the sense of separation of the various segments of the novel. But the four parts of *Charles Demailly* do have—in the tradition of the anatomy —thematic coherence, and again the theme is that of a pessimistic view of the reality that lies behind a cheery illusion. Let us examine the "novel" once more from this perspective.

The opening chapter shows the editors of *Le Scandale* concocting an unknown story that, when published, will claim to be real. This action is quickly followed by a conclusion: "Each of these *enfants terribles* was hiding a man and a purpose" (11). For instance, Mollandeux seems witty and Parisian on the outside but is really bourgeois inside; he would like to retire to the provinces and play the role of a country squire. Nachette is always dreaming about an ideal but is never able to be satisfied by his real achievements. Couturat seems jovial and friendly but nurses a secret desire to own his own paper. "In this man, there was inner laughter designed to show his mask and to hide his face" (19). Couturat works like a mole toward his goal while laughing, joking, and punning on the surface (22). Malgras is a perfect hypocrite, always preaching duty, church, honor, and morality, but one gathers that in truth he is a man who is attracted by evil and full of repressed lust (23). Bourniche does not even have an inner *Moi*; he is but a series of exterior metaphors and imitations of others. Disgusted with the Parisian scene, one character, Florissac, is eager to reveal the filth and the lies behind the facades of the great. Like the Goncourts, he even toys with the idea of writing his memoirs (34). Like its editors, the newspaper pretends to be a responsible journal of opinion but is exactly the opposite.

The low estate of journalism, we are told, was the result of a new literary ambition in the nineteenth century—to make letters into a trade or a vehicle for acquiring wealth. Under the *ancien régime*, men of letters did not have to sell out to mercantile interests (this view of the past was seriously oversimplified) and therefore could concentrate on leading public opinion. Now, as the Goncourts put it trenchantly: "Do you want the ethic of *Les Hommes de lettres* in a nutshell? A book is a gentleman, the newspaper is a whore." [12] This "lowest trade of them all," as Demailly puts it (4), only reflects the larger corruption of all society. The Goncourts insisted on the quality of illusion and reality: "What offends me, and makes me vomit, are the lies and lack of logic [of the bourgeoisie], whereas all held together under the *ancien régime*." [13] Yet this very hypocrisy of the times generated their own counterthrust of energy, their own desire to tell the trugh about it. [14] This desire to protest never left the Goncourts. A remark made years later, in 1889, showed what their fiction was all about. Edmond wanted to write a book, *not* a novel, "a book in which I can spit on my century, a book whose title would be *The Lies of my Era*." [15]

This desire to excoriate their times naturally led the Goncourts to intercalate essays about their society into their fiction. As is common in the spirit of the anatomy, they often have no direct bearing on plot development. Their function is to expose the evils of the times where men in power keep public opinion from rising to the heights. All opinion is turned into curiosity, becomes calumny, slander, low anecdotes, envy, and the washing of dirty laundry in public (26). There are other essays on the costs of the book trade, the life of writers, critics, Paris itself, women, and the Bourgeoisie. All combine to paint a portrait of society given over to false values while maintaining the illusion of virtue. Viewed in this light, they are not irrelevancies.

The final "essay" of this first part of the work takes the form of Charles's own journal, some sixteen pages in all, entitled "Memoirs of my Dead Life." The pessimistic tone, already clear from the title, is deepened by a sense of *fin de siècle* decadence that marked the period from 1850 to 1900. The Goncourts felt the same sense of racial debilitation that they attribute to their hero: "Of a sickly and delicate nature, coming from a family in which were fused the sickly delicacy of two races of which he was the last offspring," he has a "nervous sensitivity" that could sense any moral flaw, no matter how seemingly well hidden. He can penetrate any mask, and the truth that he finds behind the facade has made him melancholy, although he expresses it through irony rather than through tears (72).

The hero's only antidote to the hypocrisy of the age is his dedication to Art, an idea already suggested in *En 18* . . . In the opening chapter there is a brief appearance of the novelist Champfleury (under the name of Pommageot), whose ponderous literary doctrines the Goncourts did not admire, but even so Charles says of him with respect: "He works and he believes in what he does" (41).

The pages of Charles's journal, as well as those of his creators, make clear that the masses can never understand art, that this dedication to it is possible only for an elite. As Charles puts it in a direct quote from the Goncourts' *Journal*: "If, with this *artistic* sense, you work to achieve *artistic* form, if to the idea of the form you have the form of an idea, then you won't be understood at all!" (82). When the lonely artist Charles finds a handful of fellow believers with whom he can commune (i.e., the second group of men of letters), the Goncourts stress that the contrast between the two groups is not only a matter of talent but also involves the basic idea of personal integrity and genuineness: "Charles found himself at ease in this world where each showed himself as he was and thought out loud." A sense of "frank openness replaced all the affectation and pose" (134). Here for the first time there is honest and intelligent criticism of Charles's novel. Thematically, of course, the new group serves to highlight true values by being an exception to the prevailing world of cant, illusion, and hypocrisy.

The relationship between Charles and Marthe and, in a larger sense, between men and women is a different subject but the identical theme, for the experience of Mario Uchard and Madeleine Brohan was typical, not exceptional, in the Goncourts' opinion. The *Journal* is studded with derogatory comments on the fair sex. Behind the facade of beauty, they believe, there lurks a "little hysterical animal which can be brought out by champagne."[16] This creature of sensation is morally bankrupt: "This sense of injustice, of prodigious bad faith, of peevish teasing, pitiless and cowardly, [is] in all women." This violent condemnation is "proved" by the following entry: "It is so true that women have a genius for the false, that they can grasp everything but Truth, that they have never given an historian to the world."[17] With such a vision, it is not surprising that their ideal of sexual relationship was to have woman come in once a week for their physiological needs. The only woman that they truly wanted as a mistress was one without any pretensions to culture—these aristocrats liked slumming.[18] They even protested that the popular picture of a woman destroyed by the dull incomprehension of a husband, which Flaubert had made famous in *Madame Bovary* (1857), was very one-sided. "In the present-day household, the woman is certainly the solvent which destroys the character and honor of a man."[19] This is precisely the thesis both of *En 18 . .* and of *Charles Demailly.*

The theme of illusion and reality in women is built up with some care. In an early chapter at the Opera Ball, Couturat and Demailly discuss the eternal problem. Nachette has just gone off with a woman "masked to the teeth" (62) and Couturat comments: "It's annoying; I know all these women. . . . There is nothing worse, Demailly, than to recognize everyone at the masked ball. I'd just as soon recognize nobody." The symbolism of the masks is obvious. There is in the novel one exception to the general rule that women are false. The salon of Madame Mardonnet pleases Charles, for here he can find "women with the attitudes and freedoms of men [*femmes garçons*] who are freed by their own frank character from convention, lying, pettiness and prejudices of their own sex, and who speak their minds" (55). A place like this, conclude the authors, is the only gathering place for true men of letters, who need to flee the "comedy of learned propriety, of bourgeois cant" (56) and to have a genuine interchange of ideas. But women like "these" are not the type one marries, conclude the prejudiced Goncourts, and hence the rule for any artist is that celibacy is necessary for thought (191). Because women are beautiful and men are weak, Charles violates his own precepts by falling in love with Marthe as he watches her acting on the stage, where the real person is disguised in a play role, an image of the traps of life. They then meet at the masked ball, where again the real person is disguised; then they are married.

The Goncourts describe very ably the raptures of the honeymoon. They use traditional symbols by means of a tapestry that in a delightful eighteenth-century style announces springtime, dawn, and uses the colors rose, gold, and lavender. It is the portrait of the

ideal, but the Goncourts make it clear that the Watteau-like setting
is "the most delightful lie" (204). The reader is hardly surprised,
for Marthe had already told how as a child she had stood on a bench
to reach for grapes, and the bench broke. Charles had commented:
"One always ends up by breaking the bench" (200). From this point
on, everything goes to pieces for the hero. Marthe mishandles
money, is narcissistic, and above all cannot understand *art*. She
wants her husband who is working on a play to use a hack collaborator to insure a greater popular success by the use of formula
writing, and her ideal in literature is the fiction of Paul de Kock,
because his works "at least have a plot" (227).

Under her persecution Charles begins to show signs of mental
instability, and in an attempt to save the marriage, the couple goes
off to the country. The setting allows the Goncourts to incorporate
nature directly into their fiction. In *En 18 . .* a description of Bas-
Meudon had been so charming that reviewers then and now have
singled it out for praise. But the Goncourts intended any description
to be functionally integrated into the work: "The description of
things and places is not in the novel, as we understand it, description for description's sake. It is the means of transporting the
reader to a certain milieu favorable for a moral rejection, one which
must spring from these things and places."[20] In *Charles Demailly*
the use of nature is ironical, for the Goncourts establish a contrast
between the beauties of nature and the horror of the human situation. In the rustic setting, nature is idyllic, the castle they rent is
charming, with woodcuts representing all the seasons in an idyllic
mode (258). A kind of Edenic woods surrounds the place; all should
be in happiness, were it not for the final sentence of the chapter:
"It was on the day that they were returning, laughing as they
walked, that they saw, abandoned by a path, a broken racket, whose
handle still had a trace of red leather, the skeleton of a dead play-
thing, the only memory of yesteryear." This ironic scene prepares
the tone of a discussion that follows, in which Charles's doctor
explains the weakness of modern man, with his overworked nervous
system and his hyperexcitation, the pervasive degeneration of the
race, and the collapse of all society. These decadent motifs are
given precisely at the moment when "the sun sank to the horizon,
abandoning [the world] with regret" (261).

In the succeeding chapters the beauty of nature alternates with
scenes in which Marthe torments her husband to keep him from

recovering from his illness. The human picture becomes increasingly somber as the natural beauty is intensified. As they are about to return to Paris, there is a final vision: "He let his gaze become lost in the luminous mist of an autumn morning. It was like dawn floating in a cloud. All was mist. A thousand rays caressed with blueish whiteness the rosy trees and silvery river. Here and there a branch covered with dew shone in the sun like crystal and Charles for the last time embraced with his heart and eyes this sky, this water, and these bare trees which had seen the last beautiful days of his love."

This disparity between nature and human well-being prepares us for the final duplicity of the plot (Chaps. 75-82). Nachette and Marthe play an underhanded game in which they appear innocent; Couturat who foils their scheme does so, as we said earlier, out of a desire to gain control of the newspaper. Charles is destroyed by the accumulated hostility. His madness develops as the exterior world ceases little by little to exist for him, and the inner world into which he unconsciously takes refuge breaks up into fragmented, hallucinatory visions. There is a complete reversal of illusion and reality, for the exterior world has now become illusion for him and the interior one a nightmarish reality, as was the final dream of the similarly named Charles in *En 18 . . .* In *Charles Demailly* too, the hero hears the mocking laughter of a woman (366), and while we are spared the horrors of his inner nightmares, we get one final glimpse of an attempt to convert his world of demons into something beatific. His last desperate written page is an apocalyptic vision. He sees himself in a laundry where angels are washing souls clean and then the souls climb a ladder to dry out on heaven's clothesline (364-65). Illusion may have become reality to Charles, but the reader recognizes that an escape into madness is no good solution.[21]

Despite the harsh judgment of all critics, the merits of the novel are numerous. It is unified and carefully elaborated on a thematic basis. The world of letters and of journalism is explored by people who knew it well and who convince us of the accuracy of their picture. The dialogue is very well handled, and while some novelists (such as Flaubert) caution against too much dialogue in fiction, any technique is successful if one can get away with it, and the Goncourts do. There are interesting innovations that vary the style, with some chapters in the form of letters, one as a diary, and one even as a play taken from a newspaper (a thinly veiled parody of Charles and Marthe's life together). All this should spell success, but there is a serious flaw. While the Goncourts always claimed that art and style were their main concerns in writing, and while they insisted on the function of their work in exposing the evils of their day, they also wanted as *hommes d'analyse* to capture human reality, to give a sense of "real" human beings. Here they fail with both hero and heroine.

We mentioned above that Marthe is based on a real person, but what is true is not necessarily true to life. We are convinced when Marthe reveals her stupidity, but there is no explanation of her viciousness to her husband whom she loved when they were married. The idea that she carries her roles as villainess over from the theater does not solve the problem, for it is merely stated, not built up minutely through watching her in her professional life. As the action of the novel hangs on this point, the flaw is serious.

The hero too is unbelievable, although for different reasons. We have no idea of what he looks like, no idea of his early years. Where Charles Bovary in Flaubert's masterpiece is revealed through physical description and early humiliation, Demailly floats in a vacuum. He has no past, no family to situate him; even the world of letters is shown often as apart from him. And time itself is a problem, for the novel is shattered into ninety-four chapters which present vignettes without continuity, a technique acceptable in an anatomy but awkward for a novel. Hence no organic growth seems feasible for the hero. Further, given the importance of the central theme, the hero tends to become a vehicle for the theme to a point where he becomes too abstract (although less so than, say, in Voltaire's *Candide*).

Novelistic fictionality is threatened by encroachments from the world of ideas on the one hand and that of society on the other. But despite its inadequacies, *Charles Demailly* was a clear signpost for the Goncourts' future efforts in the novel. When discussing the stupidity of women, the two brothers attributed it primarily to the hypocritical upbringing that bourgeois girls received. This idea that people are formed by their milieu, while hardly a novelty since Balzac, would permit the Goncourts to solve a central problem: how to integrate the theme of the individual with the society from which he emerges. Henceforth, the "anatomical" quality, already reduced after *En 18 . . .* , would become increasingly a minor aspect of their fiction, as the Goncourts adapted themselves increasingly to the traditional forms of the novel.

II   Soeur Philomène

The world that the Goncourts had explored in their first two works of fiction was their own familiar world of letters and of art. After 1860 they seemed to need a change and it was, paradoxically, the world of letters that provided it. They and Flaubert had by this date become friends, and while dining with him and Louis Bouilhet on February 5, 1860, the latter told them a story which was to be the kernel of a new novel. The story told of a nurse, a sister in a Rouen hospital (Bouilhet was an intern there at the time), who felt a platonic love for another of the interns. This man hanged himself, and while Bouilhet was keeping vigil with the body during the night, the sister entered the room, knelt and prayed a full fifteen minutes by the bed as if Bouilhet were not even present. When she rose to leave, Bouilhet gave her the lock of hair which had been destined for the dead man's mother. The nurse took it without a word and left, and she never alluded once to what had happened. What struck the Goncourts in this incident was the gentle pastel quality of the nurse's unspoken love, and they referred to the tale as "cette jolie nouvelle"—that lovely story of a sister in the Rouen hospital.

But the finished product projects no such roseate glow. As Edmond later commented: "One doesn't write the books one tries to. Chance gives you the initial idea. Then, unknown to yourself, your character, temperament, moods, what is in you that is the most independent of yourself, bring the book into being. Fatality, an unknown force, a will superior to your own, control the work and guide your hand. Sometimes, as for the novel Soeur Philomène, the book which leaves your hands doesn't seem to have come from you. It is alien to your world, your milieu, your usual ideas, your entire social personality. It surprises you as something that was in you that you didn't know about." Jules was still more somber: "The strangest book we've done, a book that is not personal at all, lugubrious, heart-breaking even more than horrible. It's like a corpse on our table. What is this book? I really do not know."[22]

The essential explanation for the sharp difference between this work and their previous efforts is that the new vogue for Realism had caught up with them. One recalls their admission that they had no central vision of humanity, with the result that their characters seem to float in a vacuum. But already in Charles Demailly the basis for a different concept of characterization was emerging, when they explained the nature of middle-class girls by their upbringing. There was nothing new in this idea, for in 1842 Balzac had written in his *avant-propos* to *La Comédie humaine* that people existed in a milieu like animals in a habitat, and the differences between them were due to their habitat and their occupation. But after 1855, Realism came into its own. Champfleury (whom we saw above in the person of Pommageot in *Charles Demailly*) had expounded the new esthetic for several years, and in 1856 he and Duranty published a newspaper called *Le Réalisme*. As of 1855, too, Hippolyte Taine based his career as a critic on the idea that man is explained by his race, by the period in which he lives, and by the milieu that he inhabits. These ideas at first horrified official critics, for they seemed to imply to the conservative mind that man was not a divine origin but rather that he was just another animal. But partly because of the increasing vogue for scientific explanations of phenomena and partly because of the success of *Madame Bovary*, the new movement gained some degree of acceptance. The great critic Sainte-Beuve, who like others had had a negative first reaction, swung over and joined the Realists. The Goncourts, who had disliked him since 1857 because he had been harsh on their historical works, now were able to effect a rapprochement. They sent him a copy of *Soeur Philomène*, and the critic praised it for its realism: "It is a novel which gives the perfect truth, directly studied from life."[23]

The Goncourts rejected the view that realism should be a flat imitation of reality (Champfleury had once praised a writer *because* he was insipid) and held out for fine writing and unusual effects. But they did accept the principle that man was formed by his milieu and, in the positivistic tradition of Auguste Comte, believed that he could be studied with documented rigor. Later as the "Realistic" movement became "Naturalistic" they added to this importance of milieu an insistence on physiology and its impact on the nervous system, and hence on psychology—an idea already visible in their portrayal of women. Moreover, their training as historians led them further into the practice of documentation. Hence it comes as no surprise that Edmond and Jules were seriously interested in exposing life as it was in a city hospital. Flaubert, whose father was a doctor, arranged letters of introduction, and late in 1860 they visited the Charité Hospital. On December 18 they followed the chief surgeon Velpeau on his rounds, and on December 23 and 26 they spent a few more hours observing night duty, the operation of the clinic, and the interns' lunch. They were later to brag in the *Journal* that "we must truly have remarkable powers of observation. The public, I mean the literate public, will never believe that we could have described the hospital as we have after only ten hours on the spot."[24] Documentation meant, of course, people as well as places. Consequently, the Goncourts provided a careful, lengthy development of the heroine in a sharp change from their previous works of fiction. They wished to show how the girl became a nurse on the basis of temperament and upbringing. This lengthy introductory part of the novel is therefore anything but the "interminable preamble" that Fosca complains of.[25] Quite to the contrary, in a convincing manner the Goncourts create a real girl, give a direction to her life, and prepare her for the facing of its reality.

Their point of departure was Rosalie Doumergue, the niece of their own servant Rose Malingre. Four years old when her mother died, she was taken in by her aunt, and then put *en pension*. The Goncourts learned the details of her life through Rose, including how in the convent school the girl had a mystical correspondence with a friend.[26] The rest of the novel seems to have been imaginary except that, as Ricatte surmises, they poured much of their own delicate sensitivity into their heroine.

Marie Gaucher is a young girl of the lower class who is orphaned at an early age. She is sheltered for a time in the household of a Madame de Viry and is cared for by an aunt who is a domestic there. In this home the heroine acquires the aristocratic tastes and sensibilities of her milieu and even falls more or less in love with the young master, Henri. The Goncourts are preparing their favorite theme: the child, unaware that social mores make it virtually impossible to change class, becomes victim of the illusion that she is a true lady. But reality intrudes. The adults come to realize that she is operating on a false premise and send her away to a Catholic orphanage. When she enters, even her previous name is stripped away (they give her the name Philomène), and she must start again to build her life.

In the subsequent chapters she alternates between acceptance of her new reality and inability to cope with it. In showing her very human struggles, the Goncourts reveal the emergence of the senses, particularly as she approaches puberty. The Church tries to impose an illusory education made up of pious legends, miraculous apparitions, and the like. A friend, Céline, accepts this teaching and with her delicate nervous system becomes a mystic: "beside and above real life, these thoughts, these reveries had become Céline's blessed life" (37). For Philomène this teaching plus physical maturation coincide with her first communion. Her religious yearnings are presented scientifically, explained by isolation, fasting, poor food, the nervous irritation of constant prayer, as well as by age and formal instruction. What her system really longs for, the text makes clear, is marriage. Eventually she moves beyond an ecstatic state of religion; her exaltation disappears, and she returns to Madame de Viry's house. Here the young man, now mature, does not even notice her presence. The destruction of this final illusion about her role in the world forces her in a more practical direction. A nurse can be a kind of mother. This profession will be her reality.

When the scene moves to the hospital itself, we find confronting the heroine another aspect of illusion. She has naïve views about this noble calling and has romanticized its ugly reality. To emphasize this idea, the Goncourts created an initial chapter (actually the first of the novel because the heroine's early years are revealed in a long flashback), showing the nurses making their rounds by candlelight at night. The darkness emphasizes a world apart, cut off from the world of Paris outside, where the patients' moans announce the theme of suffering that is so important to the pessimism of the text. The skillful contrast of blackness and light produces great dramatic impact, as seen in the following passage: "In the thicker part of the darkness, at the end, at the very end of the hall, a tiny gleam flickers, a point of fire appears. A light, emerging from the distance, walks, grows, like an isolated light in the black countryside toward which one heads at night. The light comes nearer, it is behind the big glass door which closes off the ward and separates it from another; it outlines the arch, and it lights up the glass, the door opens, one can see a candle and two women dressed all in white" (7-8). After presenting this shadowy world of darkness and light, the Goncourts introduce the problem of perception of reality. In the first two pages one finds the words: "appearance," "seem," "doubtful," "appeared," "uncertain." All are used in the context of physical darkness, but have a larger sense. The nurses who bring light and life seem to comfort the patients, but at one moment when Philomène is about to make a poultice, a voice cries out: "I don't want it—I don't want it" (10) because of the pain involved. This first negative reaction prepares the nurse's next encounter. She comes to a bed whose curtains are closed and hanging inert. A corpse lies inside. All the nurse's light and compassion cannot prevail against this finality. The contrast is heightened (a bit too obviously) by juxtaposing the joyous cries that one can hear from the nearby maternity ward (12) where "it seemed to her, in these cries and wailing of the new-born, that she heard life itself crying out." But lest one assume too confidently that life has overcome death, that silence is defeated by human expression, the Goncourts dispel this cheery illusion by closing the chapter in brutal fashion. A scream followed by tears comes from a sickbed; a doctor pushes away the inexperienced nurse Philomène who disappears into the darkness.

This prologue is followed by detailed elaborations of the illusion-reality theme in hospital life. First we overhear the interns' conversation in their duty room. In the *Journal* the Goncourts had transcribed exact dialogue that they had heard on their brief visit, and some of it appears without modification in the text—more than realistic, it is real. But the brothers modified it to bring out the main point: to show doctors as they really are, without idealization. We observe their wit, their slang, their professional judgments. The hero, Barnier, speaks of his attitude toward new nurses and emphasizes their failure to grasp reality: "I don't like the young sisters, that's my principle. . . . I hate their romantic ideas. It annoys me to see these little girls get carried away and become nursing nuns without knowing why, nor what it is, because it's like a novel. . . . The old ones, whose hand and heart are now steady, they're OK" (98).

Philomène passes through the various training phases that offer her successively more realistic visions of her chosen profession. Initial trepidation gives way to a false sense of security, then is followed by a feeling of near-nausea as the horrors of hospital life overwhelm her with their cumulative effect. Only after these stages does she emerge fully trained and able to accept reality. The authors comment about her early hopes: "It was like a dream whose vanity was exposed by time and reality . . . but when she was undeceived, when the truth appeared at the end of months of struggle and anxiety, she had become strong; she no longer needed the support or lies of illusion to go forward on her path" (111). Much of the reality in question is of course the inevitability of death in all its horror. Man tries to escape through work, love, and playacting, but he ages, disintegrates, and dies. A hospital must hide this grim reality in order to give the patients an illusion of hope that will permit some of them to recover. But a nurse like Philomène discovers "each day a little more of what the hospital hid so admirably from a first glance" (102).

After this lengthy preparation, the point of view shifts away from the heroine to Barnier, who finds himself obliged to operate on a woman who was once his mistress. In this central episode all the threads of illusion and reality are drawn together. Romaine, the mistress, who had remained for the intern a symbol of youthful love, has "fallen" from virtue and in a recent orgy with an unnamed man has damaged a breast, thus necessitating the operation. So much for the idealization of love. When they meet again they try to maintain the illusory memories of their roseate past spent in the beautiful countryside, she hoping that her beauty will not be marred by the operation, he keeping silent so that she will not learn the truth (176), and fearful of the cold steel of his own surgical kit. The horror is even greater because we know of Barnier's desire for ideal love. One evening, chatting with the other young doctors, he had loudly insisted that a doctor needed quick, brutal affairs, like an animal; but one sensed that in this crudeness, he was covering a deep-seated sensitivity. When Malivoire countered that above all a doctor needed illusion (160), Barnier called the comment nonsensical with that bluster that reveals the weakness of one's own position.

Barnier and Romaine are not alone in their difficulties of facing up to reality. As one might guess from Bouilhet's original anecdote, Philomène has been quietly falling in love with the intern. The Goncourts show the progression of a friendship that becomes more than friendship with considerable skill. At first, he is brusk and impatient. Than, as she becomes more proficient as a nurse, they indulge in the usual shoptalk. Neither wishes to be transferred from the women's ward where they meet daily—although neither realizes why. She becomes eventually a celestial figure for him (114). Her affection for him is increased by the general esteem in which he is held. Their friendship is deepened by Barnier's adoption of an orphaned child who becomes in a sense their child. The strain of an unspoken, unconscious love takes its toll on her health. She begins to suffer from headaches. When Barnier gives her laudanum to let her sleep, the drug permits the reader to learn of her repressed sexuality. Once again, the Goncourts make use of the dream technique to reveal the psyche that lies beyond the control of the conscious. The dream opens in an idyllic landscape, throbbing with invisible life; a bug begins to tickle her neck; it turns into a butterfly, then into a pair of lips caressing her; and then she experiences a painful bite. This truth is revealed only to the reader. There is no indication that the young woman has pondered or even remembered the dream. But thanks to it, we understand the change in the good sister's tone of voice which becomes harsh when preparing Romaine to accept the necessity of an operation. The Goncourts have used a very modern technique to reveal the nurse's jealousy.

After the psychological, preoperative tensions come yet more fundamental issues of life and death, for Romaine loses the will to live and dies from the operation. The Goncourts were shrewd enough to perceive the whole world of mental medicine against which the skilled steel of the surgeon is helpless. And beyond this discovery, they make another. Although she has given up, Romaine is also an animal and in her death throes fights against the end, even begs to be able to live. Of what value, the authors seem to ask, are Latin names of diseases in coping with such complexity?

The ultimate level is inevitably religious and is constantly visible throughout the novel. We saw how religion affected the early years of the heroine, but the presence of death leads to more searching questions. Barnier asks Philomène: "Frankly, don't you ever doubt when you see this row of beds, when you think of what is under the sheets? . . . Dying is acceptable—if it were only a matter of dying. But why suffering? Why sickness? I tell you there are days when I'm revolted. . . . *You* find a father to thank at the end of it all. . . . As for me, the one who poisons the life he gives, the one who tortures the body he lends . . . the God revealed in a hospital is a deaf, implacable God, a God of bronze and blood like the Christ who is hanging up there" (151).

These views reflect the authors' own. Although esthetically attracted to the art and music of Catholicism, they could not accept the doctrine. Already they had written in their *Journal*: "Can you see God making the brain of Prudhomme [symbol of the stupid bourgeois] or of ridiculous insects? And eternity? A being who will never have an end and who never had a beginning?"[27] By the time *Soeur Philomène* was written, the battle lines were drawn: "As I progress through life, I am filled with immense commiseration for man and immense hatred for God."[28] Man, they added a few months later, is like a mouse being toyed with by a cat, representing life.[29] It's all a grim fatality, they conclude. Nor did the institution of the Church escape their criticism. With some thoughtful Christians, they remarked: "If there is a God, atheism must seem to him a lesser insult than [formal] religion."[30] Jules's death in 1870 settled the issue. Edmond foresaw "the horrible solitude of himself as an old man on earth" and cried out: "Ah! *Divine Goodness*! We were right to question it."[31] But in their fiction the Goncourts avoided polemic. Philomène's answer to Barnier's question makes no pretense of intellectual disputation. She says simply: "Dr. Barnier, I pronounced my vows last Monday" (151-52). The lesson of the novel is an immense commiseration with man's suffering, as revealed by the intern's despair and death. So distraught by Romaine's death that in a moment of folly he embraces Philomène passionately, he is driven by guilt on both counts to committing suicide—his final retreat from the horrors of reality.

To judge the novel is difficult. There are flaws, some of them serious. The love drama, for instance, creates some oddities. Jules Lemaître, a contemporary critic, was astonished that the decent Barnier would assault a nun, and the fact that critics since have agreed with this position[32] means that the authors did not succeed in convincing us of this level of their character's personality. More telling yet, perhaps, are the contradictions in the text. Philomène asks Barnier to revisit the streets and neighborhoods of Paris which she used to roam as a child and to tell her what they are like now. The Goncourts seem to forget that as an orphan child at the Virys she was almost a prisoner and didn't know the city. The same was true at the school. Further, it implies that now that she is an adult she cannot get out into the streets, when in fact she is perfectly free to leave the hospital and does so on occasion, and thus proves that she is quite capable of visiting old haunts herself. The cause of this type of error is probably, as Ricatte surmises, the composite way in which her character was conceived, in her different identities as child, nurse, and woman, becoming almost three persons at times even though the Goncourts tried to give her a unified personality.[33] This effort at creating a whole character was attempted by isolating her and concentrating on her. In the school, she has but one teacher and one friend with whom we become acquainted; in the hospital, we fail to get to know any of the other nurses, and surely there must be more communal life among the female staff than what we see.[34]

Despite defects, as a novel *Soeur Philomène* shows a marked improvement over the earlier efforts. The protagonist is provided with a credible past that convincingly shows how milieu and physiology can create character. The doctor is given some motivation for his self-destruction. The Goncourts had done something new; they had roused themselves out of their normal upper-class habitat and had made a conscious effort to examine a disagreeable aspect of human society, one which is often ignored, in a scientific manner. This kind of analysis of the hospital world separated them from Balzac and justifies the label "pre-Naturalistic" for the novel.[35] But in addition, it is a mark of the Goncourts' artistry that they united this method and this subject matter with their own vision of illusion and reality, here reduced to the ultimate terms of life and death. With *Soeur Philomène* the Goncourts showed that they had evolved beyond the anatomy and had learned to handle the novel proper as a genre.

III   *The Goncourts' Style*

Before we turn to their next works of fiction, a few comments on the Goncourts' stylistic innovations are in order. First, as part of their developing *écriture artiste* mentioned in the preceding chapter they invented new words. For instance, they preferred "feminility" to "femininity" for no discernible reason, and more importantly they coined new adjectives from nouns and verbs or vice versa. An example is *arcencielé* (rainbowy) from *arc-en-ciel* (rainbow). Their syntactical technique has often been compared to that of Impressionist painters, as an illustration or two will make clear. To say in French: "One could see her white hand in the shadows," one would normally put it: "On voyait sa main blanche dans l'ombre." But the Goncourts tended to render it as: "C'était le blanc d'une main dans l'ombre" (literally, "It was the white of a hand in the shadows"). The white, now a noun, has become something like a small blob of paint on an Impressionist canvas. This word order has the further advantage of following human perception: we see the whiteness before realizing with our mind that it reveals a hand. With this technique, the Goncourts frequently achieved some fine artistic effects.

In *En 18 . .* and *Soeur Philomène* the insistence on shade of color, the result of their artistic training, is very visible, but the reshaping of syntax has just begun, although it is possible to find enough examples to see the manner in which their style was developing. In *En 18 . .* we find a typical example of an adjective turned into a noun. Describing pipe smoke in a ray of light, the Goncourts write that it was "similar to those powderings of atoms which dance by the skylight of an attic" (98), where in normal French one would use *atomes poussiéreux,* or "dusty atoms." A few pages later, a tuft of nettles is host for "mitish swarmings" rather than "swarming mites" (121). In the opening scene of *Soeur Philomène* describing the hospital ward, they refer to "the cold white of the percale" (5), and so forth. The English-speaking reader may be puzzled at the interest generated by these transformations of language, for they seem nothing very unusual, but this sense of the familiar is the result of the patterns of English syntax which have long permitted the interchange of parts of speech. It was more of a novelty in France. Although the Goncourts did not invent the technique (one can find it in Flaubert among others), they did develop it greatly. In fact they later overdeveloped it until it often became a meaningless mannerism. Jules Lemaître was not alone in pointing out that when abstractions replaced concrete colors, the effect was lost: "Et il mit une note presque dure dans le bénin de sa parole" ("He put an almost hard note in the benignity of his speech") instead of "dans sa parole bénigne" ("his benign speech") is no improvement.[36] Today the judgment concerning their style is mixed. While Stephen Ullmann in *Style in the French Novel*[37] is rather laudatory and even suggests some influence on Proust, Paul Guth speaks for most of us when he finds their constant excesses of style "irritating" ("agaçants"),[38] and we shall not examine their efforts along these lines in greater detail. To conclude: by this date the essential elements of their writing—vocabulary, sentence structure, and choice of genre—were well developed, and their following novels would show the plenitude of their talent.

CHAPTER 3

Exploring the Bourgeoisie and the Working Class

I Renée Mauperin

L ONG before the two brothers finished *Soeur Philomène*, they had already conceived of a much broader subject. It was nothing less than a study of an entire class, as indicated by the preliminary title, *La Bourgeoisie*—the title, one will recall, of Charles Demailly's successful work of fiction.[1] While there is no doubt of the Goncourts' hostility to the bourgeoisie—they hated its worship of money, its lack of esthetic taste, and its pious belief in "Progress" —their initial idea was intended to be an unbiased examination along the lines of Demailly's fiction. In his novel, Charles had shown the evolution of this class over three generations: first a grandfather, a peasant type who acquires land, who is hard on himself and others. Like the peasants of Zola's future novel *La Terre* (1887), he is indifferent to any lofty ideals. The flowering of this class would take place in the next generation, represented by a father, a noble soul, patriotic and honorable; but the third generation, the son, would be decadent and degenerate, skeptically representing the aridity and calculation of self-interest, the disintegration of moral fiber under the impact of the temptation to make a quick fortune.[2] The women of the family also come under scrutiny: the grandmother, mute, dominated by her husband (as in Balzac's *Eugénie Grandet*), the middle generation showing a virtuous wife and ideal mother living by the side of her admirable husband. Then the daughter, a modern girl, who may be personified in two forms, one mannish and neurotic, a kind of perverted creature of the type that swarmed through the decadent literature of the *fin de siècle*. The other possibility for the daughter would be more attractive, a girl who had the freedoms of a man and yet retained her femininity. The didactic purpose of showing this rise and fall was to explore through "psychological drama" the "moral catastrophe" of this class.

But by the time Jules and Edmond settled down to writing their own novel, this initial plan had been considerably modified, as seen in the title changes. First we have the novel entitled *La Jeune bourgeoise*, suggesting the shift from the class to an individual typifying it. The reason for the change was rather personal. After 1855, the Goncourts became close friends of Louis and Blanche Passy, and Jules even fell in love with Blanche in a delicate, platonic way. Hence the desire to make her the heroine of a work of fiction. The titles continued to particularize the heroine, first *Mademoiselle Mauperin*, and finally *Renée Mauperin*. This increasing individualization did not entirely please the elder brother, who grumbled in an 1875 preface to the novel that the plot was only secondary and that he really wanted to change the title back to *La Jeune bourgeoisie* but that it was too late to "debaptize the volume."

The result of these changes in focus were twofold. First the grandparents disappeared from sight, and with the concentration on the third, or youngest generation, the parents no longer held center stage with their energy and virtue. All the characters as they appear in the novel became more complex than the original simplistic scheme had outlined. The situation is as follows: M. and Madame Mauperin, well-to-do bourgeois, are trying to marry off their daughter Renée. She rejects all of her dutiful and dull suitors and is the despair of her mother. Renée's brother Henri, on the other hand, is an *arriviste*, trying to make a wealthy marriage, and even manages to marry the daughter of his mistress, one Madame Bourjot. But triumph for Henri turns into disaster. He had taken on—at the Bourjot's request—a noble name which was thought to be extinct, but a last survivor is alerted by Renée herself, furious at her brother's machinations. The surviving aristocrat kills Henri in a duel, and the shock of this indirect murder is so great that Renée dies.

The intricacies of the plot show the Goncourts' desire to be more traditional in their fiction, conforming to what is expected of a novel, but even so, the narrative events are still secondary, as Edmond emphasized in his 1875 preface. Sociological dissection and character analysis of the heroine are their main concern, and the real strength of the novel is that these two seemingly disparate elements are smoothly fused into a whole. The opening scene of the novel— as startling in its way as its counterpart in *Soeur Philomenè*—shows this technique admirably. The conversation begins: "You don't like the social whirl, miss?" In her answers, the heroine Renée can reveal both herself and society (*le monde*). Her young suitor, "correct" in every way, utters only cultural platitudes, whereas Renée, a prisoner of her sex and of class propriety, fulminates against social customs. It isn't proper for a girl to read adult books, not proper for her to want to talk with educated men rather than clucking with the other hens. This conformism even applies to painting; she does oils, whereas a girl should limit herself to watercolors. Her language is bold; she admits that she likes to eat, saying "I have a stomach." But the big surprise has been carefully prepared. The conversation takes place in the Seine River where the couple has gone for a swim. This odd fact is itself incorporated into patterns of what the bourgeoisie finds acceptable. As Renée says; "if we were at the seacoast, it would be all right to be here together. But the water of the Seine is not at all proper!"

The novel branches out after this scene to study her family and then the bourgeois class as a whole. M. Mauperin, rather heavily modeled on the Goncourts' own father, is a soldier turned politician and industrialist. He is not convincing as a social type for the simple reason that we never see him at work. In fact, the details of social background, so well depicted in Balzac, are a problem in this novel, to such an extent that Ricatte stresses the theatricality of the fiction; that is, we follow dialogue of characters on stage, as it were, divorced from a complex social milieu. As a result, M. Mauperin lacks life as an incarnation of his class, and as Ricatte shrewdly concludes: "For him to come alive, he must cease representing the Bourgeoisie, and become simply a father anguished over his daughter's illness" (221). Madame Mauperin, on the other hand, conforms more to a known type; she is the middle-class mother obsessed with marrying off her children. With unsubtle irony, the Goncourts show the "ideal" marriage of one vapid daughter happily wedded to a nonentity, the pair unconsciously conforming to all that is expected of them, in contrast to Renée who simply will not play society's game. Henri, too, is a conformist in his desire to marry for money, and his mother even consults a socialite priest who arranges such unions. L'abbé Blampoix is not a fictional invention, being a fusion of one Father Carron who arranged society weddings, and the contents of a pseudo-religious manual, *Today's Christian Woman* (*La Chrétienne de nos jours*).[3] The Goncourts use the priest to satirize contem-

porary religiosity by having the worthy father preach a doctrine
that can be reduced to the justification of all pleasure-seeking.
The women whom he guides reveal their spirituality through the
following anecdote. They complain about a wealthy courtesan who
is driving up the price of labor in the countryside by paying decent
wages. "Before her," they object, "we could do good cheaply. It's
no longer possible" (167). Perhaps the Goncourts were influenced
by Augusta Labille, the daughter of an acquaintance and the model
for Renée's sister, Madame Davarande. In the *Journal*, they complain of her socialite religion.[4] In the novel, they say of her fictional
counterpart: "She was pious: God seemed *chic* to her" (161). Edmond and Jules were revolted by "this woman, dedicated to society,
even in church and faced with the problem of her salvation." They
describe her as "virtuous, absolutely, naturally, fundamentally,
without there being in her virtue any effort, merit, or awareness."

These women spend their lives attending art exhibits, teas, re-
ceptions, and the like. As these events were the activity of married
women, one can imagine the importance of the nuptial ceremony.
For Renée's sister, "marriage . . . was a carriage, diamonds, livery,
invitations, acquaintances, the ride in the Bois de Boulogne. She had
all that, had no children, and was happy. Three dances every evening, forty calling-cards to distribute before dinner, running from one
at home to another, having an *at home* of her own; outside of this
life, there was for her no possible happiness" (160). This social life,
whether of the men or of the women, had one constant aspect to it.
It was all sham, all convention. Even if Renée's sister accepted the
system so unconsciously and so fully that she has become her
society's values, still she is false because the society is inauthentic.
By this technique the Goncourts have made a crushing indictment of
a society that produces such soulless characters leading empty
existences.

Another aspect of the life of the class is seen through the brother,
Henri. The suitor of the opening scene sets the standard: "Any man
of a certain standing [*tout homme un peu bien*] belongs to a club"
(12). Henri who is seeking wealth and power joins various clubs
(alumni societies, historical societies, charitable organizations, etc.)
in preparation for a political career. Politics is a special part of the
social world and deserves some special analysis. Henri's political
beliefs are vaguely "liberal," just enough ahead of what will become
accepted government policy so that he can seem independent of the

government without really losing his privileged position. Another equally realistic type of political thinking is seen through M. Bourjot, the epitome of the nouveau riche. Under the conservative Bourbon Restoration (1815-30), as a draper's son he had been a Republican, almost a revolutionary, even to the point of actively conspiring against the crown. After 1830 he calmed down but continued to be hostile to Guizot's bourgeois regime which, as he saw it, oppressed the people. But the popular upheaval of 1848 terrified him now that he had become a wealthy landowner. "He fled to doctrines of law and order, turned back to the Church as if it were a police force, and towards the divine right of kings as an absolute of authority that could guarantee the value of his holdings" (112). He was now a legitimist who paid for portraits done by the classicist Ingres, and he fulminated—in vulgar popular language—against the masses who no longer knew their place.

While the Goncourts were themselves legitimists, they were not fools, and they present Bourjot's views with considerable sarcasm. As we stated earlier, they saw with increasing clarity the evils of their society based on money to the detriment of human values and came to realize that changes would be coming. Through their mouthpiece Denoisel they forecast with considerable accuracy some future trends: "There was a revolution against the nobility," he says calmly to Bourjot, "there will be another against wealth. They guillotined the great names; they'll suppress the great fortunes." Bourjot riposts with a defense of laissez-faire capitalism, emphasizing the equality of each person before the opportunity to rise in the world. Industry, like man, is free. Denoisel, suggesting that many industries are actually not open to all and that circumstances often prevent an able person from rising, sees ahead of his time. His conclusion: "Just between us, I don't know whether the bourgeoisie is the last word in social structure," and for Denoisel and the Goncourts the objection to it is probably more esthetic than ethical. Bourgeois domination does not "elevate the soul," and now that the working class does not believe in the felicities of an afterlife, it will want more in this one. Bourjot concludes the satiric chapter by agreeing with Denoisel on this last point: "We must make sure that the rabble go to mass." (208-12).

Against the politico-social backdrop of this society is silhouetted the drama of Renée. As this novel is the second consecutive work of the two brothers to have a woman as the central figure, and as this was to be the pattern for all of their remaining fiction except for Edmond's *Les Frères Zemganno*, one must ask why there was this concentration on women by two misogynists. They confess themselves through Denoisel:

In the midst of the monotony of venal loves, he had developed not a keen desire for adventures, but a great curiosity concerning women. He had set out to seek the unexpected and the unknown in them. The actresses all resembled the same courtesan, the courtesans all resembled the same actress. What attracted him was the un-pigeonholed woman [*la femme non classée*] . . . . He often went at night wandering about the streets, irresistibly drawn by one of those creatures, neither vice nor virtue, but who walk prettily in the mud. . . . His vocation was to discover muddied stars. From time to time, he picked up one of these marvels of nature and of working class, had it talk, looked at it, listened to it, studied it; then when he was tired of it, he threw it back into circulation. (201)

There is honesty here but also a frightening egoism, not to mention a staggering condescension toward women and the working class. As to the attitude of Denoisel toward women as a sex, the *Journal* confirms every utterance that he makes. Surely one may—one must—suspect latent homosexuality here. Perhaps for that very reason the presentation of Renée is captivating. The woman studied in this novel is not a *demimondaine* nor a *grisette* but a virtuous girl in whom sexuality is hardly awakened. As Denoisel has no desire for women, he and Renée can develop a deep, always interesting friendship that is expressed in sprightly dialogue that avoids conventional language and really tries to grapple with human relationships, art, and ethics.

But a troubling question arises: If women are formed both by biology and society, how can Renée escape the inauthentic existence of all the others? Denoisel explains that the majority of the French have decided to put an end to creating girls who resemble dolls on a string, trained to be ignorant of everything. Now people want a girl to be personal and natural. She can talk; she must be able to talk about anything. Now mores demand an original intelligence. Into this new climate Renée was born, and in addition, she has been spoiled by her father and has been given a maximum of freedom. This greater freedom furthers her authentic development. She approaches, then, the Goncourts' ideal as expressed in *Charles Demailly*, of a man's mind in a woman's body.

There is quite obviously a contradiction here, however. If every girl is breathing the air of a new freedom, why does it affect only Renée? To answer this question, we must remember that the period of Renée's formal education dates from 1845 to 1850. This period, in fact, had none of this new freedom, relying still on the old traditions in women's education. The changes were introduced later and were becoming visible in the 1860's. Her education is therefore something of an anachronism; the Goncourts superimposed onto a conservative structure of the 1840's a more modern character who was inspired by the 1860's. Renée is an amalgam of two young women. One was the Blanche Passy referred to above; the other was one Blanche Jouvin, daughter of Villemessant, the editor of *La Presse*. The *Journal* of March 27, 1862, speaks of Mlle Jouvin in terms that apply perfectly to Renée: "A charm mixed with slightly boyish pranks, expressions, grimaces, pouts, shrugs of the shoulder . . . all things that make of her something very different from girls who live in the world of high society, [they are] personal beings who reveal frankly their likes and dislikes. Girls who bring to the social world the freedom of language, the boldness of being of a woman in a domino mask, and also girls in whom one sees at heart naïveté and candor, a loving openness which the others lack."[5] In other terms, the brothers put into their heroine the qualities of a few rather unique Parisian girls, and by the time they added their own attitudes—Renée does not really love; like the Goncourts she examines and studies love as a clinical spectator—she emerges as a fascinating person but as too much of an exception to be a credible type of the modern girl of 1855.

There is another aspect to the heroine that keeps us from believing in her human and social reality: her death from heart disease. With their growing awareness of things medical, the Goncourts believed and would have us believe that her death is medically credible, and it is true that they read and annotated Coursart's *Essai sur les maladies du coeur* and Bouillaud's *Traité des maladies du coeur*. Renée is healthy at the beginning of the novel, but the heart damage is supposed to be the result of the shock she receives when she realizes that she has caused her brother's death, and the Goncourts believed, as we do not, that emotion can cause *direct* and *immediate* physiological damage of this type in a healthy girl (179). Further, once she falls ill, as Ricatte observes in his admirable destruction of the medical pretentions of the authors, her death is very decorative. One might even say that her death has a decided literary flavor (only slightly disguised by medical terminology) reminiscent of many another heroine dying of a broken heart. Once again the Goncourts have inadvertently flawed their novel, which is in many ways a superior creation. But even so, *Renée Mauperin* gave the Goncourts the chance to ponder class attitudes. During the period from 1862 until the novel's publication in 1864, the Goncourts were preparing themselves to handle a major event in their lives, one that was to result in their finest literary creation.

II   Germinie Lacerteux

For years the Goncourts had been blessed with an ideal servant, one Rose Malingre, who had lived under their roof and who was part of the family. She had known Jules since he was an infant; "she was a girl who lived our life, who opened our letters when we weren't there, and to whom we could tell our affairs. When I was young, I had played with a hoop with her, and she bought me apple tarts with her own money," wrote Jules, adding that she would collaborate in the escapades of Edmond, slightly older, who sneaked off to the Opera Ball, thanks to her secret assistance.[6] The years passed, and in July, 1862, when vacationing at Bar-sur-Seine they little suspected the blow that was about to fall. They were working on *Renée Mauperin* but cut short their writing and returned with Rose to Paris, for she was very ill from pneumonia. She died at the Lariboisière hospital in Paris on August 16, 1862. Her death was in itself a considerable shock, for the Goncourts had been close to her during her illness, even to the point of placing suction cups on her to stimulate the circulation.[7] These physiological details were unpleasant for two somewhat squeamish bachelors, but more importantly it made them realize the precariousness of even their well-regulated world. Her death reminded them that no world, even their restricted one, can last forever. She would not be there to close Jules's eyes in death as she had been there to buy tarts for him in life.

But her death was to be followed by another shock. Within a few days of her passing, a hideous truth was revealed. Creditors began to appear to present bills for debts that she had incurred by drinking absinthe and brandy to excess. Next Maria, Jules's mistress, who was of the working class, revealed a more abysmal truth. Rose squandered her money not only on liquor but on men, in particular on a young boxer named Alexandre Colmant, whose mother owned a nearby creamery. To provide her lover with money, Rose had stolen from her masters.[8] Colmant had made Rose pregnant but had refused to marry her. When the child was born, Rose was briefly happy, but the baby died in infancy. Repudiated by Colmant, and spurred by a growing nymphomania, she had taken men of the lowest kind, even paying for her needs. She died—ultimately—of pleurisy, the sequel to the pneumonia which she caught standing all night in a cold rain watching the home where Colmant was spending the night with another woman. The fantastic aspect of the whole affair was that all of it—nymphomania, alcoholism, theft, pregnancy, and poverty—went on under the supposedly observant eyes of the Goncourts, and they never suspected a thing. Their surprise, as one can imagine, was immense. Ricatte is understanding, for he concludes: "that two men, absorbed in their work and their friends, should pay very little attention to the oddities of a servant who had almost seen one of them born, and that this almost maternal quality put her beyond suspicion, this one can accept" (267). But not all critics have been so charitable. The burden of their accusation is that the aristocratic Goncourts were so anti-working class that they did not truly look at people of a lower social order. Even more, Rose (and in fiction Germinie) is merely an appendage to the bourgeoisie. No wonder, they claim, that Edmond and Jules did not see the truth; for them Rose was not an authentic person. Harsh as is the indictment, it contains some truth, as is easily shown not only by examination of the authors' social attitudes but of their esthetic ones as well.

In 1853 the Goncourts had written a very small volume entitled *La Lorette*, a compilation of vignettes of a certain type of prostitute. There is in this early volume a first association of sexual promiscuity and the working class. This vision was to be reaffirmed in 1877 when Edmond wrote *La Fille Elisa*, and in between, in 1865, *Germinie Lacerteux* associates a working-class girl with nymphomania. There is a kind of titillated voyeurism or slumming on the part of the Goncourts as they peer at the *peuple*, as they themselves admitted: "Why should one choose these milieux to study? Perhaps because I am a well-born man of letters and because the people, the rabble, if you will, holds for me the attraction of unknown and undiscovered populations, something of the *exotic* which travelers seek."[9] Another aspect to the problem is revealed by the Goncourts' delight in the refinements of eighteenth-century art. In this *Journal* they had written: "We seem to be emigrés from the eighteenth century. We are . . . contemporaries of this refined, exquisite, supremely delicate, adorably corrupt society, that is, the society farthest from a state of nature that the world has ever seen."[10] This language is the language of the decadents of the late nineteenth century in that it stresses the corrupt. As they explained in 1866, "the passion for things does not come from the pure goodness or beauty of these things. One adores only corruption. A man will have a passion for a woman because of her whorishness [*putinerie*], her evil, or a certain scoundrelly quality of the head, the heart, or the senses. One becomes passionate [in matters of style] for a certain gaminess of vocabulary."[11] With these tastes in mind, we can understand their comment in 1866 that "one must be an aristocrat to have written *Germinie Lacerteux*."[12] What appealed to them in their heroine was implicit in the following description of the troubled times before the French Revolution: "At the end of a society, when there are no more doctrines, schools, when art is between a dying tradition and another which is beginning, one can find unusual, prodigious, free, changing, decadent, adventurers of line and color, who mix everything, risk everything, and mark everything with a seal that is singular, corrupt, and rare."[13]

With these views, it is easy to see how the Goncourts have been criticized for their attitudes on the working class, and one would suspect that their portrait of their servant would be in the tradition of the decadent novel of J.-K. Huysmans, *A Rebours (Against the Grain)*. It ought logically to, but it does not. First it begins with a ringing preface, one justly famous, that views the working class with dignity and respect. It is worth quoting extensively because it marks the first major realization that the novel must henceforth be open to the third estate, and here the authors expressly repudiate (and the text of the novel bears them out) their own decadent, erotic desire to titillate:

We must beg the public's pardon for giving it this book and we must warn readers of its content.

The public likes false novels: this novel is a true one.

It likes novels that seem to take place in the world of high society: this book comes from the street.

It likes salacious little works, memoirs of whores, bedroom confessions, erotic dirt, and scandal with its skirts lifted in bookstore showcases. What it will read is severe and pure. Do not expect a decolleté photograph of Pleasure: the following study is the clinic of Love. . . .

Why have we written it? . . .

Living in the nineteenth century, in a period of universal suffrage, of democracy, of liberalism, we wondered whether what we call the "lower classes" did not have the right to the Novel; . . . we wondered whether there still were . . . in these years of equality, classes unworthy, misfortunes too lowly, dramas too foul? . . .

These thoughts had made us undertake the humble novel of *Soeur Philomène* in 1861; today they cause us to publish *Germinie Lacerteux*.

Now . . . that the novel has broadened its scope and is becoming the great, serious, passionate, and living form for literary study and social investigation, and is becoming through analysis and through psychological research, contemporary history of mores, now that the Novel has imposed upon itself the study and the discipline of science, it can claim the liberty and freedom of science. Let it seek Art and Truth. Let it show the poverty that the fortunate of Paris must not forget; let it show to high society what the social workers have the courage to see . . .: human suffering. Let the Novel assume that religion which the previous century called by that vast name of *Humanity*.

This ringing proclamation sounds more like Hugo or Zola, believers in progress and champions of the downtrodden, than the utterances of snobbish aristocrats. It is also studded with words borrowed from science like "étude" (study) and "enquête" (investigation). The use of scientific terminology had started with Balzac's comparison of humanity with zoological species, and soon Zola was to quote as an epigraph for his *Thérèse Raquin* (1867) Taine's motto that Vice and Virtue were products like vitriol and sugar. During these same years Darwin's *Origin of Species* was translated into French (1862). Even history and religion came under the spell or the scientific method, as Renan's shocking *Life of Jesus* (1863) attested by its demythologizing of the Nazarene. This general atmosphere of the scientific disciplines surely influenced the Goncourts as they in turn were to influence the younger Zola. But whatever the cause, one must recognize that two snobs, two aristocrats, despite some condescension, did their utmost to penetrate to the center of a person of the working class. In a sense they had to justify —although belatedly—their reputation as clinical observers, if only after the fact.

In writing *Germinie Lacerteux*, they had to revise their previous practices. First of all, there was the heavy temptation to describe their protagonist simply as a *débauchée* hiding behind a hypocritical mask and thus deceiving her masters. This vision would have fit in neatly with the patterns of *En 18 . .* and *Charles Demailly* concerning illusion and reality. But both the more thoughtful exploration of personality that they had undertaken in *Soeur Philomène* and the years of close frequentation of Rose made this facile answer unacceptable, and so they tried to make sure to seek a more profound truth, an intention clear from the preface with its language of "true" novels versus false ones.

Another change that they needed to make was in the concept of time. In their previous fictional works, especially the first two, the two brothers had presented life as a series of essentially discontinuous tableaux with the result that often the characters seemed a bit shallow, for they were not anchored in a developing historical tradition of a family or a society. But in the case of Rose, the continuity of her being was thrust on them by the fact that she had lived continuously with them over the years. Time was in this case inescapable and provided the skeleton for a good novelistic structure. We have seen that in the earlier efforts the action was packed into one explosive incident, but much of the rest of the work did not seem to be telling a story. In *Soeur Philomène* they started with continuously developing time when telling of the heroine's childhood, but the novel eventually disintegrated into vignettes and tableaux at the hospital. In *Germinie Lacerteux* time is maintained quite well throughout, permitting the exploration of the development of personality, the authors' chief aim.

The Goncourts started with a set of assumptions concerning their heroine's social background and physical temperament. In an early exposition of her childhood (rather mechanically done, and the only real weakness of the novel), we learn of her peasant origins, her early poverty, and the death of her parents. Coming from this background, she learned to accept as almost normal a life of hard work in which others exploited her. The Goncourts were not afraid to shock their contemporaries with realistic details: for example, when she came to Paris to live with an older sister, she arrived covered with lice. To emphasize her lowly status, the Goncourts create a contrast with her employer, not two bachelor brothers, but an old maid, Mlle de Varandeuil, whose life, ruined by a tyrant father, shows that exploitation and anguish are not limited to the working class. But at least she does not live in abject poverty. As to the psychology of Germinie's employer, "[she] had been calloused by time and her own existence. Her heart's exterior was as hard as her body. Never complaining, she did not like to hear the complaints of others. And because of all the tears that she had held back, she detested childish tears in adults" (46). She thus develops a "virile" nature whose insensitivity will prevent her seeing that her servant is living a life of debauchery on the side.

Germinie arrives in Paris, works in cafés, and is generally neglected by her sister and her family. Raped at the age of fifteen, she drifts from job to job until entering the service of Mlle de Varandeuil, in whose home she becomes a fixture. The whole series of episodes points to her role as passive victim of society, and like Hardy's Tess, victim of fate. But "fate" in this novel (as often in the Naturalistic school) takes the form of physiology. Taking the tendencies that had been emerging throughout the century and boldly carrying them a step further than they had in *Soeur Philomène*, the Goncourts proceeded to give a physiological explanation of character, one that under the circumstances of her life would lead her to disaster.

First, of course, she is a woman; and for those misogynists, all women have something "feverish, shivery, sensitive, and wounded about them, an anxiety and the desires of a sick person calling for caresses of language like a child asking for its nursemaid's song. She needs as much as a lady of high society, to be able to confide and to pour out her troubles. The nature of her sex is to confide and to lean on another" (44). Then the Goncourts add to this basic fact a lymphatic temperament, which implies sluggishness of thought and action. But in one area, there are possibilities for intensity of experience: all women need love and maternity, the authors reason, and therefore her life need not be a dull one. Even before she falls in love, "emotion showed in her eyes with the heat of a fever, pleasure with the flash of a kind of intoxication" (52). The first area where love is likely to be found by a working-class girl is religion and the Church. The Goncourts remind the male intellectual community in an interpolated essay that the Roman Catholic Church is and will remain strong because it alone provides an outlet for the emotions of the working-class girl. The priest in his confessional "is the only one to seek out her effusions and to worry about her mental health,

the only one to lift her above a material life, the only one who can
touch her." Germinie has this normal experience, which not only
reveals her basic emotionalism but also helps to mature it. Next,
finding that this expression of love can go only so far (a priest rejects
her when she seeks out the man in him), she abandons religion, but
the emotions are still there, ready to explode. The novel's opening
paragraph underscores her emotionality. When her mistress recovers
from a serious illness, Germinie is so grateful that "she began with
a frenzy of happiness and a fury of caresses to kiss . . . the old lady."

The diagnosis is simple: Germinie is suffering from *la mélancolie
des vierges* (virgins' moodiness). By the age of twenty-four, still
sexually unsatisfied, she has an "ardent, irritated, poignant desire
for marriage." But she is not lucky. As Emile Zola was to write of
her case, "give Germinie a decent husband who loves her, let her
have children, take her out of the milieu of easy vice, let her legiti-
mate needs be satisfied, and she will remain decent."[14]

While speculation about nonevents in fiction is inherently useless,
the comment does point up Germinie's bad luck. Outside the comfortable home of Mlle de Varandeuil lies the "real" world. Daily
the servant woman does the shopping, and she also uses it to satisfy
her psycho-physiological needs. For lack of a husband, she begins
informal adoptions of children. First, she mothers a niece for awhile
when her sister dies, and then when the child leaves Paris, she starts
to "mother" the son of Widow Jupillon who runs the nearby creamery. When the boy grows into a young man, Germinie falls in love
with him (as Rose had with Alexandre Colmant). The love, exacer-
bated by jealousy, for the Goncourts add to her equation the fact
that jealousy was inherent in her nature, has a powerful effect on
her. The following passage is characteristic of what has become
known as Naturalism—the attempt at a scientific explanation of
humanity, particularly of the lower classes: "This joyous but unsatisfied love produced in Germinie's physical being a singular physiological phenomenon. One would have said that the passion which
flowed in her renewed and transformed her lymphatic temperament. . . . The miserable nervous energy which sustained her had
given way to healthy activity, a noisy, bustling, overflowing joy.
Her former weaknesses, depression, prostration, fatigue, laziness
were gone . . . and all day long she had the same good humor of the
body, the same gayety of motion" (71-72).

The implications of this passage are twofold: (1) character depends on physiology, an attitude of the new Realism-Naturalism that clashes sharply with the tenets of both Classicism and Romanticism; and (2) a real change in personality is possible. The Goncourts were trying to deal in a new and more profound way with their old theme of illusion and reality, as the following passage suggests: "sometimes, what she had lived seemed dead; the sensations of being that she had felt until then faded into the depths of a dream and to the bottom of a sleeping memory. The past was behind her . . . " (72). Germinie has the illusion of being liberated from the past into a heavenly existence only to learn progressively that her new life is, in fact, hell on earth. She abandons any bargaining power with Madame Jupillon, a syrupy hypocrite, and with the son who is a scoundrel. The mother merely wants someone who will work for nothing in her shop. Love, on the young man's part, had been only the "satisfaction of a certain evil curiosity, seeking in knowledge and possession of a woman the right and pleasure of despising her" (87). Bullied, neglected, and scorned, the more she sacrifices for her lover and his mother, the more she is rejected. Pregnancy brings her temporary relief, but as she must conceal it from her mistress, her very joy is darkened, and she must go through the ordeal of serving a meal while in labor. One may question the idea that an old maid with good eyesight would be deceived, and there is a general critical view that the Goncourts transferred their own myopia to Mlle de Varandeuil.[15] Germinie's stocky build and bulky clothing are not quite adequate to explain this oddity.

Despite her successful attempt to disguise the pregnancy from her mistress, Germinie is still dogged by bad luck. Her lover takes up with a pretty cousin, and her baby dies. These events seem to mark her future. She feels powerless to resist the evil influences that possess her, as she puts it. Jealous of her rival, and with her guardian angel (the baby) no longer present, "a radical change occurred in this morbid, extreme character, which had no middle ground. . . . Poisoned for a long period of time, love turned into hatred. . . . " She became persuaded that Jupillon had killed the child (125).

So still another being is created in the heroine. Rather than a simple mask and reality, there are multiple realities: Germinie the victim prior to entering the service of her mistress, Germinie the ideal servant, Germinie in love, now Germinie hating Jupillon and, so great is her despair, adding the problems of alcoholism to her character. She compounds her folly by going into debt to buy an army replacement for Jupillon (although she hates him, she cannot keep from giving him everything, so strong is the sexual attraction). Soon she loses any control of herself as, sunken in alcohol, she begins having nightmares and hallucinations. Her work as maid falls off badly, and she steals to pay pressing debts. Here the Goncourts pause to have Germinie wonder "whether she is indeed still the same woman" (166). The answer is, of course, that she is at least two real women at once: "She led something resembling two lives . . . , succeeded in separating them, living them both without mixing them, and not letting the two women in her get confused" (113). Hence she is still a devoted servant; she does truly love her mistress. No hypocrisy is involved; there was no mask for Mlle de Varandeuil to peer behind.

This idea of multiple personality is shown by use of a mirror image. About to steal from her employer for the first time, she sees before her in the glass her own face: "she recoiled with shame before the face of her crime. It was a thief's head she was carrying on her shoulders" (171). She has *become* that thief. The progress beyond *Charles Demailly* and even *Soeur Philomène* is immense.

The novel rolls swiftly to its despairing conclusion. In the grip of the fatality of physiology (even remorse, supposedly a matter of the innate conscience, is presented as an outgrowth of her particular nervous system [158]), she never conquers her nymphomania, first taking another lover and finally offering to pay men in the street. "What was left of resolve, energy, courage, melted away under the feeling, the desperate conviction of her powerlessness to save herself. . . . Fate was crushing her, and Germinie lowered her head beneath its foot" (193). There is in this ending the purifying sublimity of tragedy. Ricatte goes to the length of concluding that by becoming the total victim, she closes the novel purified, in a sense and dies definitely chaste (258). This is perhaps a misreading, for Germinie is chaste only from illness and necessity. The pessimism of this novel derives from the knowledge that her absolute destruction has served no purpose at all, and no one is saved by her act of surrender.

This bleakness is worked out in the details of imagery in two particularly remarkable passages. In the first Jupillon and Germinie are headed to his mother's where Germinie will decide to borrow money to save the young man from compulsory military service:

Both began to walk, each by the other's side, without saying a word. They

arrived at a paved road which stretched out endlessly between two lines of
street lights, between two rows of twisted trees thrusting up into the sky a
handful of dried branches and silhouetting on large flat walls their thin,
still shadows. There, under the sky, sharp and icy from the glare of the
snow, they walked for a long time, disappearing into the obscurity, the infinite, and the unknown of a street which always follows the same wall, the
same trees, the same street lights, and leads to the same night. The heavy
damp air that they breathed smelled of sugar, soot, and carcasses. On
occasion, their eyes were dazzled by the light of a delivery van which revealed disemboweled animals and hunks of bloody meat. . . .

This passage, both sensitive and precise in its detail, shows the Goncourts' power at its best. As a premonition of the heroine's life it is
also clear: the absence of communication, the sameness of the road
of life, the gathering night of death and oblivion, with the dead
carcasses. The passage reflects, too, the linear concept of time in the
novel in its traditional image of a street that unrolls before the characters. Although Germinie senses the truth, she cannot—any more
than we can—refuse the voyage to death. "Marchons," she says
("Let's go" [144]).

On other occasions, nature is beautiful, but only to heighten the
bitterness of existence. With the memory of her own dead child
still keen, she must watch other children at play on a beautiful day
that serves only to heighten the irony (187). Death has the last word.
A description of the pauper's grave leaves the reader with a final
vision of reality. This description has its own history, having begun
with one to be found in the *Journal* on August 31, 1862.[16] This first
version stresses the variety of colors on the sensory plane (naturally
enough, in August), the ghostly nature of the place on the level of
psychological impression, and horror at society's scorn of the body
of the poor on the moral level. A few months later, in February,
1863, Jules went back and made a watercolor sketch. The season,
the grayness of the day, and the traces of snow remove the color and
heighten the desolation. It is from this watercolor that the final
description was composed. In the novel, the grays are dominant,
befitting a scene from which life is absent. The objects described
have a systematic symbolism. First an endless enclosing wall suggests the "no-exit" nature of life and within the cemetery, bare
trees with their leafless branches enhance the gloom with their
skeletonlike forms. Both these images were present, significantly,
when Germinie accepted to return with Jupillon to his mother's

place. The images continue. The snow is a shroud; funereal cypress
trees catch the eye; the crosses are anthropomorphized into persons
in distress. But individuality is lost in death, and the names on the
crosses are obliterated by time. Mlle de Varandeuil cannot even find
a marker for Germinie's grave, for the dead are disturbed by fresh
graves before the bodies are completely absorbed by the earth. The
entire scene tells of the grim finality of death, the Oblivion of the
Poor (275). There is no relief, no rebirth. The feeling is so intense
that the Goncourts wrote: "Leaving my novel to read some eighteenth century material, I am nauseated by its dryness. Those people never suffered."[17] Even their beloved eighteenth century paled
before this agonizing picture of the grimness of reality. These descriptions fulfill the authors' hope that "a description be not just for
its own sake, but that it transport the reader into a milieu favorable
to the creation of an emotional involvement, which must spring
from these things and from these places."[18]

The Goncourts awaited publication of their novel with some trepidation. For the official press and government censorship bureaus
could cause them real trouble. Inevitably, the poignancy of the
novel was missed entirely as the conservative critics called the novel
"filthy" and "rotten." Even their friend Princess Mathilde was
horrified and wrote them in what was a typical reaction: "I read the
book without once putting it down all the way from Dieppe to Paris,
saying to myself the whole time: 'How can decent, well-bred minds
discover such monstrosities . . . and follow them like this to the very
end without insuperable disgust?' I need to believe that there are
not many Germinies and to hear you say so."[19]

But the more sensitive and astute saw the matter differently.
Flaubert exulted that they had surpassed the man reputed to be the
leader of the new Realistic school—Champfleury. Jules Claretie
felt intuitively that the novel was moving ahead in science and in
truth. The greatest impact was perhaps on young Emile Zola who
wrote the Goncourts in February, 1865, and asked for a copy of the
novel, for he admired not only the boldness but also the artistry, and
it is unlikely that Zola's *L'Assommoir* would have been possible
without *Germinie Lacerteux*. The novel is a great one, for it combines new views of personality with powerful social protest, in a
milieu described to bring out the horrors that can surround the
existence of a human being.

CHAPTER 4

Experiments in the Theater

"LORD, what a hold the theater has on people's minds in France," wrote Edmond in 1895 as he looked back at his own life and at the French literary scene during the century.[1] His exclamation was only too justified, for success in the theater was indeed the great obsession of many novelists of that era. The reasons for the prestige of the stage are not hard to find. First, there is the centrality of Paris as the one intellectual center in France. If one can dominate the stage there, one's renown radiates throughout the country, with the result that literary battles have not been uncommon, as for instance when the Romantics seized control of the theater in 1830, or in the twentieth century when Jean-Paul Sartre made it clear that he wished to use the theater to destroy bourgeois ideas. Furthermore, the lasting reverence for the great playwrights of the Classical era—Corneille, Molière, and Racine—continued to keep the theater at the top of the artistic world, and finally, theatrical success could reward the author with sudden wealth and overnight reputation. As Edmond put it in his *Journal*: "To be known in the world of letters, universally known, it is important to be a dramatist, because many lawyers, doctors, etc. don't have the time to read, but they do go to the theater."[2] Thus it was that Stendhal had dreamed of being the new Molière, Balzac had tried his hand at composing plays to earn the money needed to pay his ever pressing debts, and in the latter part of the century, Daudet and Zola among the novelists desperately wished to succeed in this genre. Even the aloof Flaubert wrote a play, but except for Daudet, none of these novelists had any real dramatic gifts (the finest playwright of the century was no doubt the poet Alfred de Musset). As for the Goncourts, we recall that their first literary efforts were in the theater.

Although they abandoned the idea of writing plays for some years, they frequently wrote about the theater in their *Journal*. After all, they saw themselves as critics of history and of the novel; why should they not touch on the theater? They, like other critics of their day, felt that the theater was at a low ebb and needed rejuvenation. There was no point in trying to revive Classical drama, which could only be a historical memory recalled for repertory theater as part of a glorious tradition. Romanticism in the theater, it was generally agreed, had died with the failure of Victor Hugo's *Les Burgraves* in 1843. As Realism was becoming dominant in prose fiction, the question was raised whether it should also conquer the theater. In fact, there had already taken place a noticeable transformation since the era of 1830. Since theatergoers were in large part those bourgeois who could pay the price of admission, plays appealed progressively to middle-class concerns. Marriage and money became the dominant motifs of plays extolling the life of the comfortable family. The weakness of this theater was that the plays were usually bourgeois morality plays, ones in which wealth and morality were reconciled in a contrived ending; and like many a Hollywood movie of the 1930's and 1940's, there was something false in the vision. In 1860 the Goncourts showed their dissatisfaction with this state of affairs, commenting: "All the plays I see are worth nothing."[3] At times, they despaired of the stage as a vehicle for artistic expression, feeling that the genre was good only for communicating sensory impressions, not complex or subtle ideas. Earlier that year they had written: "I am thinking, once again, how clumsy the theater is as a means of observation or of giving an intimate history of a society."[4] This last judgment seems a bit surprising, but in all probability only reflects the low quality of dramatic productions of the day. Despite the pessimism, however, they finally were willing to conclude that a genius could re-create a theater of characterization. On various occasions and with some differences in wording, they expressed their belief that all theater is in the construction of characters, the individuality, and the style. As for the progress of the plot, the denouement, that was of no importance. Once again we see, this time in the theater, the disinclination of the Goncourts to conceive of literary structures based on a plot line.

But when they began to consider in greater detail the mechanism of renewal of the theater, the Goncourts seemed to have only one real interest, which was to create a new style. They gave it the label of "langue littéraire parlée" ("spoken literary language"), but the phrase seemed to mean little more than an attempt to reconcile natural dialogue with a sense of beauty. But whether or not this concern contributed to any "realism" in their plays, their theater was in fact often judged "realistic." Complaining that their view had been misunderstood, Edmond in the preface to the volume of their plays put it clearly: "Basically, we failed in the Theater for the crime of being 'realists' and for having written a 'realistic' play. Well, I must explain about that. In the novel, I confess, I am a convinced realist; but in the theater, not at all" (15). "Actually," he went on to say, "we thought we were creating modern fantasy" (16). This dual interest—in Realism and in its opposite—showed up frequently in their *Journal* commentaries. Writing of Greek art, for example, they complained: "Frankly, what is it? The Realism of the beautiful. No fantasy, no dream. The absolute of line. Never a grain of opium, so sweet, so caressing to the soul."[5] In a similar vein: "As one writes . . . one says one day—'There's only observation.' And then the next day, observation strikes you as insufficient. Something else is needed which should be in the work like a bouquet in a wine."[6] This vacillation was not, of course, apparent to the theatergoing public, as Jean Ajalbert wrote in the postface to the volume of theater in the Edition définitive: "They were labelled novelists, and novelists they were to remain" (306). And as novelists they were known as "Realists," and so their plays must—logically—also be realistic.

I   Henriette Maréchal

This misunderstanding of the nature of their theater was to be compounded by an extraordinary cabal when their first major play, *Henriette Maréchal*, was produced at the Comédie Française on December 5, 1865 (it had been written in 1863 but had lain dormant in the author's desk since that time). The play had passed the censors' watchful eyes on December 2, although the director feared that certain daring lines might cause vocal objection during the performance. But already an attack was being organized against the play, and for reasons that had nothing to do with esthetics. Students from the Latin Quarter lined up for opening night, prepared to boo the play. The reason for the hostility was that the Goncourts were known to be anti-Republicans and intimates of the salon of Princess Mathilde, and it was supposed that because of her influence the play had been imposed on the Comédie Française. The premiere was a stormy one indeed. But after the initial difficulties, things began to go better, and the sixth performance was performed in complete serenity. But at this juncture an attack was mounted from the opposite camp. On December 17 the play was banned, and the blow apparently came from Empress Eugénie, who was an enemy of Princess Mathilde, at least according to Jules, who expressed his conviction of this intrigue in a letter to Gustave Flaubert on December 21.

The Goncourts were overwhelmed by all the uproar. How could they be associated with the imperial regime, they wondered, when they themselves had been haled before a magistrate in 1852 for alleged violation of the press law? Of course they were friends of the princess, they commented, but so were all the distinguished writers and intellectuals of France at that time (except those few, like Hugo, who had gone into exile rather than serve a tyrannical state). Today's reader and critic finds it difficult to understand why this play should cause such turmoil, but the fact is that it did and was withdrawn; it was revived successfully only years later, on March 3, 1885, at the Odéon.

What was this play that aroused such animosity, that was accused by journalistic criticism of being filth which befouled art, written by authors who were later to reject explicitly Emile Zola's naturalistic theater, and whose Realism on the stage meant only the natural portrayal of human feelings ("langue littéraire parlée"). Frankly, as Edmond was the first to admit, *Henriette Maréchal* tells a conventional plot with every conventional stage gimmick known. There are two brothers, the older, Pierre de Bréville and the somewhat adolescent Paul, whose relationship, incidentally, more than suggests that of Edmond and Jules. At the Paris Opera Ball, where Paul goes for the first time, he sees a masked lady and falls in love with her. Later that evening, he finds himself involved in an argument about her and commits himself to a duel over her honor. In Act II, we discover that he has been wounded in the duel and has been transported by the long arm of coincidence to the house of Monsieur and Madame Maréchal, the latter being that very masked lady in whose defense he had fought without even knowing her name. When Paul recovers from the wound, he and Madame Maréchal discover each other's identity and become lovers. Henriette, the daughter, also falls in love with Paul, and the tension grows. Eventually the suspicious husband returns unexpectedly, surprising the lovers, but in the darkness M. Maréchal shoots his daughter by mistake. His wife's reputation is saved because the girl dies saying that Paul was *her* lover, a fitting way to close a conventional, imitative plot, for this final scene owes much to the old Romantic melodrama of Alexandre Dumas, *Antony* (1831), which also has a final act of moral sacrifice.

There is novelty in *Henriette Maréchal*, however, and it is concentrated in the first act at the Bal de l'Opéra. The scene is in the corridors outside the loges where masked figures appear, throw out a snatch of conversation, a query, a joke, and disappear. In the effervescence of the language and in the absence of any plot development, it is easy to recognize Jules's sparkling style at work, but over and above the innumerable verbal sallies of strollers there arises the clear feeling that the masks worn by the participants of the ball are intimately connected with that important theme of illusion and reality that we have seen pervading the Goncourts' fiction. The artificial posturing by the unknown strollers, the feverish gaiety of the carousing create an almost allegorical impression of masked beings acting out their roles on the stage of life, dedicated to the pleasure of seduction and set in motion by false protestations of love. We see harried husbands looking for their wives. It is here in the arena of life, full of illusion concerning the realities of love, that Paul comes face to face with life for the first time, and "life at your age, is woman" (64), says his brother. He has the illusion that something monumental and stupendous will happen, as is always the case with the dreams of exuberant youth. Against this illusion the older brother responds with the voice of experience: "My friend, nothing happens; the world is as flat as a penny. . . . Chance is dead" (64-65). But Pierre realizes that youth must learn the hard way and tells his younger brother to go ahead and sample "life." At this point a witty gentleman arrives on stage, and in his remarks are concentrated the sharpest comments concerning the illusions of love and marriage, as he notes that the revelers do not even seem to be having a good time, that the carnival will be over at dawn, and that Lent will grab them all by the collar. Yet he admits that although life seems to be worth little, we cling to it because it deceives us (69). This bittersweet tirade prepares us for Madame Maréchal's appearance, and it is in this context of the futility of existence that the idealistic Paul soon has a duel on his hands.

The theme continues to be elaborated in the rest of the play, despite the reversion to a more traditional technique of staging. In Act II when Paul is convalescing at the Maréchal's, the dialogue is designed to say one thing and to mean another, as both mother and daughter love Paul but are obliged to hide it in order to conform to accepted social standards. Paul, too (when still unaware of the identity of his hostess), contributes to the theme, admitting that to have risked his life for an "illusion" may be madness, but it is "more beautiful than life" (113). His hope, typical of all dreamers is to transform illusion into reality. The rest of the play appears designed to test the wisdom of this view of life. When Paul and Madame Maréchal become lovers, they think that their love is hidden from everyone, but the reality is quite different. Soon all of Trouville is gossiping, and only Pierre de Bréville's strenuous efforts at covering the culprits' tracks have made the illusion last as long as it has. Finally even the husband comes to suspect the truth.

Maréchal is not a typical cuckold of farce, and neither is he a stupid, ponderous businessman interested only in profits—like John Bull in Alfred de Vigny's *Chatterton* (1835). The Goncourts take pains to show him in a rather sympathetic light, and he gives the impression of being "real." Although portrayed as a self-made businessman, who has known poverty and is now wealthy, this wealth has not made him callous. He accepts and exercises his social responsibilities, and he treats his employees well. But even he, firmly anchored in reality in one sense, is living with one great illusion: that of his wife's fidelity. When he learns the truth, his bubble of happiness bursts, and tragedy strikes through his attempt to kill his wife and with the death of his daughter. Although there is a certain banality in the details of the eternal triangle up to this point, there has been a coherence of development. Act I presents as a kind of overture the current social conventions which are mocked in the setting of a world of illusion (the Ball); Act II then tests the motto that "Love Conquers All" in "real life"; and finally, Act III reveals in the final tragedy the failure of the effort of the two lovers to find happiness in a love that ignores social conventions. The only flaw in the structure seems to be the dying daughter's heroic act of protecting her mother's reputation. In a play that preaches the wisdom of social experience over the folly of youth, it would have been more in keeping with the theme to have the whole truth known, all masks removed in the final disaster.

Despite the human interest of the play, *Henriette Maréchal* has not really survived as a landmark in the history of the theater. Not only the contrived ending but also the basic plot itself lacks originality, and as for the "langue littéraire parlée," the Goncourts never really defined it; and despite their claims, it never did develop into a new theatrical style. It is true that the innovation of the masks in a comtemporary setting seems to anticipate much mid-twentieth-century theater (e.g., Pirandello, Beckett, Genêt), but because the Goncourts' popularity faded, the play was lost sight of and never did have any influence on modern drama.

II La Patrie en Danger

Undaunted by their failure, the two brothers tried again with a historical play set at the time of the French Revolution, dealing with the fall of the Bastille, France's struggle against the allied coalition, and the Reign of Terror. The play's original title was *Mademoiselle de Rochedragon*, but this title had to be changed when a genuine Rochedragon came forward to protest the use of the family name. They substituted for it the far better title of *La Patrie en danger* (1868). The subject matter was a timely one, for talk of war with Prussia was already in the air, and it is no coincidence that Prussia was the enemy selected as a foreign threat to France in their play. This theme of foreign invasion furnished the Goncourts a chance to demonstrate their chauvinism. The hero exclaims at one point: "Foreigners! just the name . . . foreigners in the streets and in our homes! Foreigners as victors, sovereigns, masters. Their language ordering where once the French tongue held sway" (277).

The play was refused by the Paris theaters and was not produced until 1875, despite its timeliness, for the reason that it is a very bad play judged by any standard. But even so, it is worth more than a passing glance because of its effort to treat the theme of illusion and reality on the stage in the context of a large historical canvas. The result was a play conceived as a series of tableaux, each of which treated a different facet of a political or social illusion.

Act I takes place just before the storming of the Bastille in July, 1789, and stresses the naïve illusions of the aristocracy, unwilling to believe that their little illusory world of privilege can crumble. As indication of his escapism, the Count of Valjuzon drinks too much and argues in his defense that "without wine, one would see

life as it is, sad, gray, dull, and flat" (185). But their life as a class is
so inauthentic that they cannot be really human. Even the Countess
herself in an obvious reference to Marie-Antoinette deplores the
playacting of the nobility when "great ladies disguise themselves
as milkmaids and lords dress like their coachmen." At the end of the
act, they learn that revolution can be real, that their artificial life
can be swept away by the events of history.

Act II continues the portrait of the aristocracy. It takes place on
the night of August 9 and the early morning of August 10, 1792, the
day of the storming of the Tuileries. We learn that the Valjuzon
family has been energetically disseminating royalist propaganda by
means of a clandestine press kept in their own house. Despite the
new Republican government, the Royalists have had and still have
hope that the *ancien régime* may be saved. But history is pitiless; at
the end of the act, they realize that the monarchy is lost; the Count
goes off intending to die fighting, the Countess is so crushed that
she cannot even pray.

The Goncourts do not limit illusion to the aristocracy, however.
The hero of the play is one Perrin, a commoner who rises in rank
to become a general in the armies of the Republic, and who believes
in the courage and virtue of the citizenry of the nation. He first
appears in Act II to try to save the Valjuzon family, who had brought
him up as a child, by warning them that all their subversive activity
is known, but he becomes centrally important in Act III when we
find him as the commander of the Armies of the Republic in September, of 1792, at Verdun. Perrin's illusion is his belief in the courage and virtue of the citizenry. At Verdun he is disabused as the
inhabitants of the city demand surrender to the enemy to avoid destruction by bombardment. Perrin opens the act by urging the timid:
"Have confidence in the patriotism of these inhabitants asking for
arms." But he learns that they are cowards and traitors (to use his
own terms), and he attempts suicide.[7] As if cowardice were not
enough, in Act IV Perrin learns that the supposedly virtuous Repub-
licans can butcher helpless civilians (249). The last significant character is a fanatic Jacobin named Boussanel, who had once been a
priest in residence in the Valjuzon home. His illusion is that of
creating a utopia, and since he has a dark side to his nature, he has
the illusion that a nation can be purified by the guillotine.[8]

All these characters are finally brought together in Act V in a
detention hall prior to execution at the height of the Reign of Terror.

About to be guillotined, they suddenly all become equal, as in a certain sense, men are all equal in the face of death's reality. Their illusions can now be seen in the light of man's true nature and of the tides of history. The aristocracy is gone; humanitarian idealism (Perrin) is shown to be naïve; and even Boussanel is there, for he discovers the reality that the revolution can feed upon its own. But curiously the play does not end despairingly, because in the face of death all the characters find a deep human dignity and even a common bond in their differing visions of a better world.

The reconciliation of class differences is symbolized by Blanche's and Perrin's confession of love just prior to execution, as it is also expressed somewhat differently by the old Count, who urges solidarity in the face of foreign nations, and who wants quarrels to be exclusively among the French, "en famille," as he puts it (255). Perrin has no bitterness toward the revolution that he has championed, exclaiming: "May the Republic live and may I die! I have lived long enough. I have done my job and my duty, I have served liberty" (285). Boussanel answers Perrin's noble utterance with one of his own. As he puts it: "Revolutions make mistakes. . . . So what? What does one life, one man matter? . . . a pebble in a torrent, nothing more, nothing more than the individual who is created by nature and then crushed for the good of the species" (286). Perrin loves life and the worth of the individual; Boussanel loves death ("death intoxicates me" [287]) and sees man as a mass. But all find their truth when faced with the guillotine. In terms of the theme of illusion and reality, the lesson seems to be that when one confronts death, illusions are destroyed, and this better awareness of one's true being brings wholeness of vision and acceptance of death itself.

The considerable difficulty that the Goncourts experienced in putting their most valid theme into a historical context, however, merely highlights the fact that theater requires more than truth and history. For characters so disparate to be able to interact requires that they all know each other and find themselves together in moments of testing and crisis. As a consequence, verisimilitude is strained, for it is unlikely that Perrin and Boussanel, who play the roles of major historical figures, would *both* have been in the Count's household in earlier years only to meet later at crucial moments in widely scattered places. Further, the fanatic Jacobin and the cynical old nobleman are rigidly stereotyped and thus weaken the attempt at "real" characterization.

This stylization of character comes from the basically rhetorical nature of the play, as revealed not only by the title but by Edmond himself in the 1873 preface, when he declared *La Patrie en danger* to be a "voice with which a national theater could whip up patriotism in France" (163). Therefore, one is all the more surprised to read in this same preface the gloomy prediction that the play will probably be refused by the theaters because "the times are no longer willing to accept attempts at pure art." In fact, *La Patrie en danger*, although written in collaboration with Jules, shows Edmond's tendency to become impatient with fiction as such and to move in the direction of social analysis. It also shows in its discontinuous *tableaux* the same lack of desire for the steady flow of time and narrative that is visible in so much of their prose fiction.

A final footnote to the theatrical attempts of the Goncourts is in order. Like so many other novelists of the day, Edmond late in his career tried to have novels adapted to the stage. The most celebrated effort was with *Germinie Lacerteux*. In 1886 Edmond began the adaptation, and in November, 1888, the play went into rehearsal at the Odéon theater, having its premiere on December 19. The play was in fact a reasonable adaptation of the novel in ten separate tableaux, and the language and the décor were in the new "naturalistic" style that André Antoine was making popular in his Théâtre Libre (founded in 1887). Edmond even walked through the streets of Paris to try to get ideas for the details of the staging.

Once again tumult greeted the play. Some of the opposition even included a local bar owner who objected to the fact that there was only one intermission. More serious objections were to the vulgarity of language, although Edmond in his *Journal* claimed that those most vocal on this score were the whores and pimps of Paris.[9] But there were defenders as well. Edmond was delighted that Romain Rolland had found the play deeply gripping, and Rolland praised the Goncourts' "clear view of life, your pitying love for those who love and who suffer." Rolland liked above all the sobriety of expression and thanked Edmond for not sacrificing his taste in order to pander to popular desires.[10] Perhaps the fairest adverse judgment came from that indefatigable theater critic Francisque Sarcey in *Le Temps* on December 24. He hit hard at the essential weakness of the play, which is also the weakness of nearly every novel that was adapted to the stage at this time. He reproached Edmond for having cut slices from the novel, so that one sees the tableaux but not the slow progression of the emotions which is at the heart of the novel. Despite the lengthy self-justification that Edmond wrote in his *Journal* in which he accused Sarcey of idiocy and malice simultaneously,[11] the indictment stands, even though much criticism was indeed engendered by personal animus and other motives that did not touch the artistic problems involved. Edmond claimed on January 1, 1889, in his *Journal* that "no matter what the critics say, they cannot get around the fact that the two most discussed plays of the second half of the nineteenth century are *Henriette Maréchal* and *Germinie Lacerteux*."[12] The two most discussed plays, perhaps, but certainly not great ones as Edmond believed. Despite his special pleading, the Goncourts' literary efforts must be judged by their prose fiction, to which we now return.

CHAPTER 5

Their Last Two Novels

T HE year 1866, which followed the hectic battle over *Henriette Maréchal* and the furor over *Germinie Lacerteux*, was notable for two events. The first was the publication of some extracts from the Goncourts' *Journal* under the title of *Idées et Sensations*, two very appropriate words in their lexicon, for they did indeed use fiction as a vehicle for ideas and their characters are creatures of the senses. The other notable event was the death of their close friend, the lithographer Gavarni (1804-66), whose work they had greatly admired when Jules was active with his own efforts in this direction. The two brothers had met him in 1851, and the three became fast friends. Gavarni, who knew English, called them his "little boys," which phrase was transposed into French as "litre boit" (literally: "drinks a litre," no doubt of wine), as a humorous nickname. But more seriously, Gavarni's influence on the Goncourts as novelists is thought to have been considerable. For years he had been sketching different social types taken from the daily life of the capital, and in 1852 had created a comic picaresque rogue, something of a working-class vagabond, whom he named Thomas Vireloque. The Goncourts were fascinated by this and others of his creations that dealt with Parisian mores, and their interest in observing social reality closely was shaped by them.[1] It seemed to the two brothers that their friend's death in 1866 marked the end of their insouciant youth, and it was also a fitting omen for the immediate years to follow, for Jules had only four years to live. The *Journal* gives the impression that they felt that they had little time left and that it should not be wasted.

I Manette Salomon

The Goncourts chose for the setting of their next novel the world of art as it existed in Paris between 1840 and 1855. They had been planning this volume since 1861 but did not start serious work until

1865. The controversies over *Henriette Maréchal* had interrupted their work for a time; in addition, they were hampered by ill-health as Jules, afflicted since 1850 by the syphilis that would one day kill him, began to feel the loss of his creative powers. As if working against the clock, they made several quick trips to Barbizon where some of the scenes of their story were to be laid, and a sense of anguish is revealed in this entry from their *Journal*: "Never will the public know the despair of trying to write a page that won't come. . . . We wish to finish *Manette Salomon*, and we have found an enormous amount to rewrite."[2] The poignancy of the situation was even greater because both brothers seemed to overlook the venereal disease and believed that Jules's deterioration was the result of a total dedication to art itself. According to them, their innate hypersensitivity, a milieu of a decaying society, and a militant life of art all developed in them a "frightening treasure of imaginative anxiety and a perceptivity that could wound and destroy them. Senses of infinite delicacy became . . . irritated by the pin-pricks of existence. These beings, agitated, frail, and violent, these anguished artists' souls . . . one could call geniuses in torment."[3] But they managed to complete the manuscript on August 21, 1866. It was published serially in *Le Temps* starting January 18, 1867, and appeared in book form that same year.

As in the case of *Renée Mauperin*, whose title evolved from the name of an entire social class to that of a single individual, *Manette Salomon* too had its evolution in title. It was first to be called *Les Artistes*, which was then changed to *L'Atelier Langibout* (*The Langibout Studio*) before receiving its definitive title. As with *Renée Mauperin*, too, the multiple titles show the brothers' problem of trying to reconcile the broad social canvas with the intricacies of individual psychology.

As preparation for their analysis of French art in mid-century, the Goncourts logically enough provide background material on artistic trends from 1800 to 1840, beginning with the importance of Louis David. While the novel recognizes that the past is gone forever, the latter is evoked with some nostalgia through the person of Langibout himself, an old painter who runs the studio that provides the early training for a group of young artists. Patterned after Martin Drolling of David's school (1752-1817), he is shown to be a man of limited talent, but also to be hard working, honest, and a man of judgment. His personal stature conflicts sharply with that of his pupils who are described as budding nonentities of little distinction. Then the Goncourts move quickly up to Romanticism, which is also of the past—having spent its force by 1840, the Goncourts believe. It was killed, they opine, by too much bookish inspiration (20). Landscape painting had not yet come into its own (although here they are oversimplifying considerably); Orientalism appeared worn out; the only giants were Ingres and Delacroix. But the Goncourts set these masters up only to knock them down again. Ingres is dismissed as a photographer who reproduces Peruginos and Raphaels. Delacroix seems for a time to receive a more favorable judgment, but we soon learn that he cannot handle flesh or color. In the Goncourts' eyes his ability to capture motion and a feverish sense of life makes him a master, yes, but a master for a period of decadence, an era of neurosis, expressing the modern torment of mid-century (151-52).

The verdicts rendered on contemporary artists are decisive enough, but history has proved that as art critics the Goncourts sometimes failed to recognize true masters. They considered Courbet's new realism a passing fad, detesting "his stupid ugliness, his eclectic vulgarity . . . without character, expression, beauty, and life"(346). Above all, they claim unjustly, he had no style. Their preference went rather to the lesser artist Alexandre Decamps (1803-60) who in 1840 was indeed popular. "The man we resemble most is Decamps. He seems to have the same style and manner of handling light."[4] Ricatte quotes Baudelaire's observation: "Decamps liked to seize nature directly by its fantastic *and* its real sides—in its most sudden and unexpected aspects"[5] in order to suggest that this description of Decamps' art fits the Goncourts, and provides a clue to the limitations of their art as well. "Gratuitous arabesques, uselessly accentuated motions, too obvious whims of lighting, Decamps has a perpetual coquettishness that could have passed as mastery but which soon made him obsolete, just as the 'écriture artiste' annoys us today," he explains.[6] Ricatte also points out that the Goncourts overrated such other minor figures as Charles de Tournemine (1814-73) and Félix Ziem (1821-1911). On the other hand, they did appreciate the landscapists François Millet (1815-75) and Théodore Rousseau (1812-67) at their true worth. Into the context of this semiaccurate panorama of nineteenth-century art history the Goncourts try to fit their several fictional painters. Each exemplifies a given trend of the times and therefore is a type, but

each is portrayed also as a human being struggling with the awe-
some difficulties of becoming an artist, a struggle which involves
the authors with problems of portraying individual psychology.

The first of these artists, Garnotelle, is used to satirize the art
of the classical academic style of those years, and he is probably
based on such real-life figures as Flandrin and Duveau. Totally
lacking in artistic genius, he earns, by dint of hard work and by
learning to please the powerful, the Prix de Rome that the Goncourts
and the great artists of the day so rightly scorned. The young man
comes from a humble background but quickly learns the formula
for success by becoming a fashionable society portrait painter. As
he rises in the social world, he also becomes a pompous ass.
Chassagnol, who at times serves as the Goncourts' mouthpiece,
explains: "The Prix de Rome destroys individuality, and forces one
into pastiches of previous styles, totally lifeless. Rome is a Mecca
for the conventional"(68). Since the conventional here means a
pastiche, and since a pastiche is an illusion of reality, conforming to
convention is like putting on a mask: if one wears it long enough,
one can become one's own mask,—in this case an exterior reality of
success with nothing underneath. As if feeling this void, Garnotelle
on rare occasions rebels against his inauthentic existence. He feels
an urge to leave the false world of high society and to find his old
friends truly dedicated to art. In so doing he momentarily becomes
his old, more human self: "In reliving the former Garnotelle who
had existed, he suddenly became his old self" (222), a man again,
able to admit his lack of true success as an artist. But this last flicker
of authenticity soon disappears, and he seeks refuge once again in
wordly success, lost both as an artist and as a man.

A more important character is Anatole Bazoche,[7] whose problem
is almost the opposite of Garnotelle's. He may indeed have talent,
but one will never know for certain, because he fails to develop
it through his unwillingness to work, being more attracted to the
artist's life than to art itself. In the Goncourts' eyes he stands as a
symbol of the Bohemian world for which they had neither liking nor
respect. Anatole's last name is symbolic, for the "Bazoche"—a
clerk's guild of the Middle Ages—was famous for its practical joking. Anatole also spends his life playing tricks on people and be-
having like a clown. He incarnates corrosive wit which the Goncourts sum up in the word "La Blague," and which they believed
responsible for much of the weakening of the fabric of French

society. "La Blague" is not healthy humor but a "feverish, evil, almost diabolical laugh of the spoiled offspring of a civilization" (37). It mocks the masks of society, but is is a mask itself, for who can see what reality lies behind the clown's makeup and costume? Anatole's illusion is that he is an artist because he paints and leads a Bohemian existence. He even believes at one point that he has a "message." He paints a horrendous allegorical tableau of democracy and progress with Christ at its center. But the illusion has no substance. Anatole never finishes it and, haunted more and more by the figure of Pierrot (the traditional clown figure in France), in whom he sees himself, he paints it over the figure of Jesus, thus stating symbolically that his grandiose message of the perfectibility of man is only a joke—an idea, of course, dear to the hearts of the Goncourts.

Anatole's fall from the heights of art is shown in many secondary ways. The death of his ambition is captured by such episodes as his working for an embalmer (120-21), by his heading for the Opera Ball and never getting there because he is drunk (98), but above all through his alter ego, his pet monkey Vermilion, who represents Anatole's true nature. The two resemble each other to the point that, in an amusing reversal, Anatole imitates the monkey's gestures just as the monkey had copied his master. In one significant scene Vermilion even tries to paint but of course can accomplish nothing. Normally, the whole world of Anatole is presented in a comic vein, and the text sparkles with puns and jokes, verbal and practical. But the mask of levity cracks on occasion. One night at a costume ball (the theme is becoming more important in the Goncourts' fiction), Anatole, dressed as a clown, goes through a despairing pantomime of a dance, parodying the nobility of the human form that he is unable to paint. He makes himself jerk, twist, and limp and finishes by "making a gesture of reaching out to grasp the ideal as it flies by, and trampling it underfoot as a withered illusion"(250). His despair is personal, but it is presented also as a judgment on France at that period: "It was . . . not the cancan of 1830, naïve, brutal, and sensual, but a corrupted cancan, sneering and ironic" of a period of decadence.

Bitterness becomes tender grief when Vermilion falls ill. Stricken by paralysis, he can no longer bound cheerfully about. When the monkey dies, Anatole buries it in a remote corner of the Bois de Boulogne and, in a touching farewell address, imagines the monkey gone to a distant tropic paradise. But after evoking this shimmering illusion, Anatole looks at the real hole he has dug and says to the corpse: "You will find the earth very cold"(337). As he tramples the earth down, just as he had trampled the ideal in his dance, he is burying not only the monkey but "something of his old self . . . some of his playfulness was underground."

The increasing somberness of Anatole's experience coincides not only with the loss of the ideal of art but also with an increase in suffering. As he passes the age of forty, reality overtakes the illusions of Bohemian life, inexorable time reasserts itself against a thoughtless existence where days had meaning only for themselves. Health deteriorates, and Bohemians like Anatole regret "that they have been but wandering passers-by of life, camping out under the stars, outside of civilization and the happiness of other men" (417). Happiness is not the only casualty of this irresponsible life. As the Goncourts explain: "Anatole presented the curious psychological phenomenon of a man who does not have possession of his individuality" (394). Like Garnotelle, Anatole has no interior; he is a clown or a monkey's face. So strongly has he become the joyous soul of Bohemia that it seems as if no reality can destroy his make-believe, which has become his true self (395). But eventually he abandons both art and Bohemia to become an assistant zoo keeper. Among the animals he finds through the immediate presence of nature a form of pantheistic happiness "as if on an earth that was still divine . . . he felt the happiness of the first men before unspoiled Nature" (474). There is, of course, a final irony: unspoiled nature is a pathetic prisoner of "civilization." Zoos are collections of cages.

The principal character, also an artist, Naz de Coriolis, was born on L'Ile Bourbon (now Réunion Island) but has lived in Paris since a child. He differs from his colleagues in that he has real talent, a capacity for hard work, and a calling to turn these gifts into true art. After his early preparation at the Langibout Studio, he flees Paris for the Near East (leaving center stage free for Anatole's antics) to study color and light. He sends back an occasional letter, full of picturesque descriptions that convince the reader of the seriousness of his calling. When he finally returns to Paris, we find him seeking a new kind of painting, one based on the observation of nature in the open air (which Anatole had been unwilling to try), yet not a servile imitation of Courbet. While Coriolis will later praise Decamps for "dramatizing the woods and the horizon" and for having a "style"(327), he is at this point impatient with

Decamps' technique, which is limited to sharp contrasts of light and shadow. The two, he claims, need to interpenetrate (163). Decamps may be accurate for the intense light of Africa, but for Turkey, light is a continuous evaporation of pearly water. Everything shines, yet all is soft. Light is an "opalized fog" with colors like the twinkling bits of colored glass (164).

It might be supposed at first glance that this technique sounds like a forerunner of Impressionism through its emphasis on detached bits of color. But Coriolis' first efforts, which include "a shining quality, without shadow or blackness, a decor of heat, moistened with a mist of precious stones"(165), owe their origin, as does much of Coriolis' letter from Turkey, to Tournemine; as for the lighting effects, Ricatte claims rather convincingly that they owe much to the facile painting of Ziem.[8] The Goncourts never did care much for the Impressionists, and the date of composition of the novel and the years in which the story is laid preclude any discussion of this later movement. If we add to the influences mentioned above a touch of Rembrandt, the reader senses some difficulty in fitting Coriolis into the artistic evolution of his day. This is all the more true because the Goncourts have poured some of their own problems as literary creators into him. Both the Goncourts and Coriolis are aristocrats, and the former are not thinking only of their fictional hero when they write in reference to a painting displayed at the Salon of 1852: "This painting had against it the name of its author, and the prejudice—too often justified—that exists against a work signed by a noble-sounding name. The signature Naz de Coriolis . . . made one imagine a gentleman, a man of the world, an habitué of the salons, occupying his leisure . . . with the pastime of art"(174). Had the Goncourts foreseen Guy de Maupassant's popularity, they might have been less ready to suppose that a noble name was an inevitable barrier to popularity. It was their temperament and their works, not their name that explains the lack of best sellers.

Despite the multiple sources, Coriolis comes to life as a person whenever we feel him straining to achieve the absolute through art. This quest for the ideal the Goncourts themselves felt keenly and they were able to transfer a sense of urgency, even of frenzy, to their fiction. Because Coriolis sees his paintings as appealing directly to the senses rather than to the intellect, he struggles to heighten the sensory impact. Hence his preoccupation with color and light. Like the Goncourts, he even experiments with the techniques of Japanese painting, with its delicate pastel colorations. He dreams of using his new effects in painting a nude for a canvas entitled *The Turkish Bath*, and in this natural manner is Woman brought to the heart of the novel. Coriolis, dissatisfied with the flesh tones of all the models he has tried, stumbles across a perfect model, the titular heroine. While she makes possible the brilliant success of his painting, she becomes in time the agency of his destruction as man and artist.

At first, there seems to be no danger to him in the relationship. Manette is, after all, a professional model dedicated to her art. As a model, she does not even seem to be a woman but rather an incarnation of Beauty (200). While she does become Coriolis' mistress, at first it does not seem very serious on either side. But when Coriolis gives his costume ball, Manette appears in the exotic garb of an Eastern dancing girl. The costume fits her particularly well because, as she is Jewish, she has a slightly exotic air of the East in her features, and in her new garb she is subtly changed, representing no longer abstract beauty but "the seductive woman"(248). Coriolis becomes increasingly jealous and wants her to pose only for him, and because as a professional herself she admires his success as an artist, she agrees. For a considerable time they are happy.

The disaster is caused first of all by Coriolis' own weakness: "He had a basically feminine temperament, a lazy voluptuous nature that liked a life of ease and of sensual enjoyment"(160). While he fought this tendency in himself, "he lacked staying-power in his work. He felt constant fatigue and discouragement" (161). In this respect, he resembled the Goncourts to a considerable degree, and like them had resolved never to marry in order to protect himself against this secret hungering for a life of ease. The artist is a "social monster"(154), for to yield to the pleasures of the family would ruin him as an artist, he believed. Just as the Goncourts satisfied their sexual desires with stupid, ignorant women who knew nothing about art, Coriolis, the artist seeking the ideal, took Manette for what she was—a charming animal whose natural sense of elegance saved her from being vulgar.

Trouble comes into the open when Manette becomes a mother. While at first she makes no effort to cajole Coriolis into marriage, soon Manette, "apparently so detached from any desire to dominate"(344), reveals "a kind of hidden, deep, disquieting, almost menacing soul that was threatening for Coriolis' future"(313-14). With motherhood, she suddenly becomes very "Jewish," that is, greedy for money, whereas in the past she had been indifferent to it. The novel rapidly becomes a vehicle for anti-Semitic diatribes. One by one, Manette alienates all of Coriolis' gentile friends and replaces them with Jewish relatives that are nothing but anti-Semitic caricatures. Coriolis, too weak to fight her successfully, tolerates these changes. Even his son is alienated and grows up a little monster. These pages with their crude bias are repellent to any sensitive reader, but they should not blind one to a deeper meaning. At first glance, it seems as if a noble mask (Art) is removed and that reality in the form of a greedy Jewess is revealed. However, the experience in multiple personality that the Goncourts encountered in the case of Rose leads them to try to express a different view: "In becoming a mother, Manette had become another woman. The model had suddenly been killed. It was dead in her. Maternity in affecting her body had taken away her pride in it. And at the same time a total inner upheaval had secretly taken place in the depths of her being. She had renewed herself and changed her nature. . . . From the entrails of the mother, the Jewess had sprung"(351). Rather than a mask being torn off, there is clearly intended a real change of personality, although the reader may not be convinced of its truth because of the abruptness of the change and the unpleasant racism. Unpalatable as well is the implied condescending misogyny, for the Goncourts believed firmly that maternity was the only genuine emotion of which a woman was capable.

Thus there is a clash between man's noble drive to the ideal through art and the other powerful compulsion of existence, woman's drive for maternity. In this case, as Coriolis is weak, the latter dominates. He comes to learn that a woman is a "fine instrument for making a man suffer"(453). His artistic talents begin to fail, and he becomes—somewhat like Balzac's Frenhofer in *Le Chef d'oeuvre inconnu* (1831)—unbalanced on light and color. His inner despair is exteriorized one day when he suddenly dashes off a powerful sketch of an old lecher leering at a nude young girl. The lesson communicated is a clear comment on man's subservience to sexual desire, and the Goncourts also make clear that the girl's tranquil, routine acceptance of lust as a fact of life is even more appalling to them. In their eyes, the suffering of Coriolis is not only personal but symbolizes the end of a decadent, neurotic civilization.

In the final pages of the novel, Coriolis, completely subjugated, is dragged off by Manette to be married.

Apart from the struggles of the hero toward self-fulfillment, there is also in *Manette Salomon* a verbal effort to ponder man's vain attempt to grasp the ideal. Through Chassagnol, beauty itself comes under discussion.[9] Chassagnol is absolutist in his demands on an artist: "Talent or death, that's the choice," he exclaims (135). But even his talent at verbal abstraction fails before the absolute. In a despairing chapter near the end, he admits the limitations of all philosphical systems: "The Beautiful! . . . how to define it? Why does the Beautiful exist? Where does it come from? What causes it to be? What is its essence? How would I know?" He goes on to talk of beauty as the "Dream of Truth" but concludes with Hamlet: "Words, words!" He wonders if beauty even exists: "Is it in the objects or in our minds?" (467-68). No answers are forthcoming.

Like Chassagnol, the Goncourts often speculated on these matters. For them, too, art was a religion,[10] but when it came to defining it they were less than clear. Pierre Sabatier in his *L'Esthétique des Goncourt* insists that the Goncourts believed in the relativity and subjectivity of the beautiful. It is true that they were individualists and correctly felt that the beautiful was an intimate expression of the personality and that, therefore, each person would conceive of it differently.[11] As Edmond would point out in the preface to *Chérie* (1884): "Every thirty years or so, three or four men transform the public's idea and taste in literature and art and make the rising generation adore what the preceding generation detested." But as these aristocrats inevitably believed that their taste in art was superior to that of their laundress, they secretly believed that their beautiful was *the* beautiful. They had a tendency to reduce the issue at times to vulgar snob appeal: "The Beautiful is what eyes without education find abominable. The Beautiful is what my mistress and my servant woman instinctively find hideous."[12] Thus despite the fact that they recognized that each period has its own esthetic, its own beauty, they felt that underlying the vagaries of popular taste lay an eternal beauty. In a sense they are revealing yet another aspect of the illusion-reality problem. To think that one can explain beauty is an illusion, but in some way beauty is nevertheless real.

This reality of "le Beau" indicates why the multiple failures to achieve the ideal are not the only vision of *Manette Salomon*. The success story of the novel is the painter Crescent, a true artist, a stable personality who never is destroyed by the ideal that he transforms into art. By common accord of critics, Crescent is primarily patterned after the great Jean-François Millet (1814-75), the open-air painter of Barbizon, where Coriolis meets him. Crescent does not succeed by any profundity of theory. His maxims on art sound deep at first hearing, but if considered as a whole, "what he ended up saying was elusive and disturbing, like the beginning of the brain's flying off into the absurd, the irrational, and the insane" (320). With a kind of peasant mysticism (like that of Millet and Théodore Rousseau),[13] he has avoided the corrupting influence of Paris and its decadent modern civilization: "In the great movement of the return of nineteenth-century man to *natural* nature, in this intimate study of things to which old civilizations return to rejuvenate themselves, in this passionate pursuit of simple, humble, and naïve beauty of the land, which will remain the charm and glory of our present school, Crescent had made for himself a special name and place"(287-88). Crescent can express "the latent life . . . the gayety, the repose, the meditation, the mystery, the happiness or the sigh of a landscape" (289) and draw the elements together with a unified tone. Crescent, the direct painter of nature, is himself a part of nature, and therein lies his salvation. He paints canvas after canvas as if he were the power of nature itself, with no thought of public success or money, without worry or fatigue, fertile in his peasant stock as the earth itself. His wife, un-like Manette, is not a handicap but a blessing to him—perhaps be-cause they have no children. Close to the soil like her husband, she takes care of chickens and handles the family finances while he paints. Their simplicity saves them, and in the forest of Fontaine-bleau they find a true terrestrial paradise from modern industry and the suffering it brings (310-11).

But Crescent is the exception. The main thrust of the novel is de-spairing and to reinforce the dominant tone, the Goncourts have recourse—appropriately enough—to nature itself. As in *Germinie Lacerteux*, the Goncourts make good use of the traditional images of nightfall and winter to suggest failure and death. Even in the opening chapter, when Anatole shows Paris to a group of tourists, his own fate and that of Western civilization are adumbrated. The setting is twilight in the month of November, when the far reaches of the capital are described fading away into the mist, with the slate gray roofs turning the whitish fog black (10). The same suggestion of night and death appears when we are first shown around Coriolis' studio as if to suggest the final destiny of the artist's talent: "The dust-like gray of night continued to fall. The last of the light was dying among the canvasses which faded away, grew smaller without moving, mysteriously, with the slowness of the approach of death, and with that solemnity of the silent decomposition of the daylight"(150). We find a similar development with the description of a Jewish synagogue (218), the end of the summer in the forest of Fontainebleau (315), night falling over the Bois de Boulogne when Anatole buries his dead monkey (380). All these passages prepare Coriolis' final disintegration and his ultimate desire for death (380), which in a final bitter irony fate refuses him.

As for the structure of the novel, it is not unlike many of the earlier efforts in that it is composed of a large number (155) of chapters, each a tiny self-contained unit. This fragmentation leads to odd effects. For instance, Anatole is living with Coriolis when Manette moves in, yet there is no lengthy development of their relationship. When a hundred pages later Manette decides to oust Anatole, we are surprised into the realization that they had indeed been living under one roof. The Goncourts did not weave a unified tapestry. Their technique is rather more that of the mosaic, fragmented when seen close to, meaningful (in their successful works) when viewed from a greater distance.

Once again, the oddities of their technique baffled readers of that era. There was little critical commentary in the press, and much of that was unfavorable. But today's reader—if he can overcome his antipathy aroused by some of the serious defects of this novel—can appreciate *Manette Salomon* as a powerful expression of the suffering caused when a talented but weak man fails in his desperate search for the ideal.

III *Jules's Illness*

The year 1868 saw an acceleration of Jules's physical decline. The *Journal* records how the younger of the two brothers suffered increasingly from noise, as the following typical entry indicates: "Oh! the noise, the noise! I've even gotten to the point of hating birds. I would say, like the actor Debureau to the nightingale, 'Will you shut up, you nasty creature.' "[14] As the year passed, Jules was increasingly unable to sleep or to eat. "An abominable effort needed to move or to want anything . . . and we have to work in all of this infernal irritation. . . . For some time, for a long time, it seems to us that we have truly been accursed."[15] To alleviate the pain and to overcome discouragement, they would say to each other: "Let us embace; it will give us courage. And we embrace without saying another word."[16] Unable to tolerate the noises of the capital, they left for Fontainebleau and Barbizon only to experience depressing memories: "Seeing a place again is always sad."[17] In August came the decision to leave Paris and to settle in the suburb of Auteuil, at that time almost rustic in appearance. But the change availed nothing, for even here Jules was tormented by noise. For some inexplicable reason they had purchased a home close to the railroad tracks. The *Journal* notes: "For us who flee from the noise of Paris, there is the noise of a horse at the house on our right, the noise of children in the house on our left, the noise of trains passing in front of our place, rumbling, tooting, shaking our insomnia."[18] To them it seemed like a personal persecution.[19] Jules even imagined, in a moment of black humor, a man in his condition killing himself to escape noise only to find no repose in the tomb because of the noise of the worms in the grave.

IV   Madame Gervaisais

Despite the most serious problems of health, however, they did their best to maintain a literary life. Noteworthy was their first meeting with young Emile Zola. Zola had not been satisfied to praise *Germinie Lacerteux* when it appeared but had also cheered lustily for *Henriette Marechal*, had sent them his early efforts at fiction, and had written a eulogistic article about them in *Le Gaulois* in September. They invited him to lunch in December and took pleasure in this ardent young writer who shared their hostility to facile light fiction and who was eager to see himself as their disciple. They also managed to write *Madame Gervaisais*, their last joint work of fiction. Given the problem of Jules's health, it was fortunate that the entire preparation for this novel dealing once again with the phenomenon of women and religion had already been completed. The heroine was based on one of their own relatives. They had an aunt Nephtalie Lebas de Courmont, who had gone to Rome and had been converted to a mystical Catholicism that was (if we are to believe her anticlerical husband) akin to madness. The Goncourts had had as early as 1856 the idea of writing a "story about my aunt,"[20] and in that same year they made their first visit to Italy and recorded their impressions, including those of Rome in a notebook.[21] In April, 1867, they had made another trip to the Eternal City, this time with the intention of gathering background material for a new novel. As André Billy has pointed out, the *Journal* gives few details of their stay, but one entry probably sums up the essentials of their constant trips around the city, notebook in hand to study a church or a ruin.[22]

Despite the personal link with their aunt and the on-the-spot visits to Rome, much of the inspiration for their novel was provided by books. They read Stendhal's *Promenades dans Rome*, Lafond's *Lettres d'un Pélerin* (1856), and Gaume's *Les Trois Rome*, also published in 1856. The combined impact of bookish sources and direct observation is considerable in as much as two-thirds of *Madame Gervaisais* consists of descriptions. In general they follow the usual tourist circuit: Saint Peter's, the Sistine Chapel, Saint John Lateran, the processions of Holy Week, and so on. These choices seem very banal but are justifiable. The heroine, a foreigner who has arrived in Rome, would naturally see the usual sights. The point is, however, not mere tourism but the idea—carried in this novel to extremes—of the impact of a milieu on a person's character. The thesis of *Madame Gervaisais* is once again the idea that religion comes not from divine grace but from explainable causes, and the novel is the story of how this aspect of her being was formed. What distinguishes *Madame Gervaisais* from *Soeur Philomène* and *Germinie Lacerteux*, where the same problem is explored, is, first, the age of the titular heroine (she is forty years old when the novel opens), and secondly, the fact that she is far better educated than the other two. The Goncourts' thesis is that since religion is an emotional need, the educated woman comes to it as surely as the ignorant, only by a different road. Despite efforts at objectivity, however, the religion presented has a strong anti-Catholic bias. While Alphonse Daudet, no ardent believer, could praise the novel without much worry on this score, a passionate Christian like Barbey d'Aurevilly was not to be fooled: "There is not, in their entire book," he wrote in a review for *Le Nain Jaune*," a single word of insult, irony or impatience against Catholicism. Naïve minds which see only words will find this book as naïve as themselves. But for . . . those who see the light behind the words, never has there been a book where the Catholic idea has been more truly aimed at and hit. . . . They have quietly, successfully plunged a knife in its back."[23]

How did the Goncourts do it? First, they took a woman who had never really loved, who had been married to an old man who had never enabled her to spend "the hidden heat of love" (216). Secondly, they gave her a retarded child. Any mother, finding that science is basically helpless before this problem, will at least be tempted to have recourse to what is beyond nature. Thirdly, she is suffering from tuberculosis. According to the Goncourts' gleanings from contemporary writing on the subject, tuberculosis aids the development of mysticism by destroying the flesh and by reducing the brain of a forty-year-old woman to that of a twelve-year-old girl, that is, to one that is "pure" (i.e., not having reached puberty), and therefore open to the ecstasies of religion like any twelve-year-old female. Finally, the woman is presented as a devotee of a philosophy which leads her to exalt the "Beautiful, the True, and the Good," but she is vulnerable precisely because these abstractions fail to satisfy woman's pressing need for the concrete in all aspects of her life.

Having established the heroine's background and situation, they then place her in Rome and study her disintegration and transformation under the impact of this special milieu. The heroine experiences emotionally first the power of ancient, not Catholic Rome, with its sculpture and its ruins, this being already a shift from abstract speculation of Beauty to contemplation of it in concrete form. The climate, too, plays a role. The hot wind, the sirocco, awakes in her an unsettling malaise, making her unable to *think* (135) and creating in her an aching emptiness that something must fill. In case her analytical faculties might be strong enough to resist the climate, she is also subjected to the sensory bombardment of the perfume of flowers (34-35) which heighten, along with the climate, her sensory perceptivity (80). When Holy Week arrives, she is already prepared to be open to the impact of its appeal to the senses. She believes at first that her appreciation of the spectacle is purely artistic (92), but in truth it is the seed of her conversion. She tries to fight off Catholicism by filling her inner emptiness with such interests as painting, then history, and then archeology. None of these substitutes lasts; indeed they accelerate her conversion. "Monuments attracted her by that intimate, familiar charm . . . that Rome alone can give for places and things" (105), and "There is a natural conspiracy and persecution of objects that are all around one that

work together to conquer a soul" (162). Finally the ancient torsos
with their thighs and breasts, the leering satyrs, all increase her
torment and anxiety in a direct sexual stimulus. In the midst of this
critical personal situation, her child nearly dies, the result of an
illness triggered by her foolish desire to teach the subnormal boy
to read. He is cured, in the opinion of the local doctor, miracu-
lously. As the servant women have been praying for this miracle to
the madonna of Saint Agostino, the conclusion seems to be that the
intellect is bad (reading brings sickness) and religion is good
(prayer brings cure). Finally Madame Gervaisais undergoes
menopause, and the Goncourts affirm that a woman is most
susceptible to "spiritual sensations" at the "age when she starts
down the slope of life" (151).

Up to this point there seems to be nothing hostile to Christianity.
Indeed, the Goncourts were trying to be objective, but once again
they discovered that, as in *Soeur Philomène*, the creation escaped
their control: "Always the element of fate with a book. We, who
have a feeling of kinship and affinity for the Pope, we who do not
detest the men called priests, here we are writing, pushed by I
don't know what irresistible force that is in the air, a book hostile
to the church. Why? But does one know the 'why' of what one
writes?"[24] What began as a psycho-physiological study of a certain
type of woman became at times an anti-Jesuit and anti-Catholic
polemic, just as *Manette Salomon* suddenly became anti-Semitic.

The descriptions of the churches and even of the pope are objective enough. The anti-Catholicism lies in the manner in which
the Church is alleged to treat the individual. When Madame Gervaisais arrives in Rome, she has a certain number of friends, an
Italian countess, her doctor, and various other people upon whom
she calls. But when she turns to the Church, things change. Her
first contact with the clergy is made possible through a chance
acquaintance, Countess Lomanossov,[25] a fascinating creature,
intense, vibrant, and mystical who, although she makes no attempt
at proselytizing, manages to recommend a good priest if ever there
is need for one. As this priest is a Jesuit, when Madame Gervaisais
does go to him, she soon finds herself in the hands of the Jesuit
order. The Goncourts describe the Jesuits as being "like the papal
government, police-state minded, jealous, fearful, suspicious of
foreign influence, trying to surround its penitents with those
belonging to the order; working ceaselessly underground, never

tiring" (172). Just as Manette drove away Coriolis' friends, Giansanti separates her from her past. One by one her associates disappear, a Gallican prelate, the French ambassador, the Italian countess, and even her doctor, her most steadfast friend. This isolation is made possible by the change in the heroine herself, for she become so extreme in her mysticism that even Giansanti loses patience with her. She then finds an even more dominating and brutal director of conscience and confessor Father Sibilla, who takes over and pushes her into mortification of the flesh and finally into repudiation of her own child. The "reasoning" behind this last atrocity is that as the child was conceived in her pre-Catholic life, his retardation was a punishment for her incredulity, and she must reject the child as a creation of sinfulness. Sibilla quotes Luke 14:26, which exhorts one to reject even one's children to be able to qualify for discipleship. The Goncourts combat this attitude in the name of a benign nature—an unusual position for them to take—for unlike Rousseau, they believed in art, the city, and civilization. Here is their judgment on the Church: "Finally a day arrived when Grace completed the task of assassinating Nature in Madame Gervaisais. In her, the woman, the earthly being, no longer existed. The original inclination of a creature to seek the honest pleasures of existence in other creatures and in objects, its need for the affection of its fellow creatures . . . its innate tendency to combat its pain and its suffering, everything that Nature provides, with its sovereign and providential force . . . seemed to her now to be only illusion, lies, phantoms of needs and instincts. Humanity had left her" (255). Not even the return of her worried brother can save her at the end. The will to live is gone, and, obsessed with death, she dies when the pope receives her in private audience.[26] Surely, the Church in recent times never made it a policy to preach hatred of one's fellow man and one's children. Yet in the novel, the heroine even learns to hate others under priestly direction. In Victor Hugo's *Notre-Dame de Paris* (1831), an evil priest destroys an innocent heroine, but it is clearly an exceptional case, whereas in the Goncourts it is presented as if it were typical. No wonder Barbey d'Aurevilly complained.

In sum, the novel cannot be considered of first quality. Ricatte tries to make a partial defense by showing that the detailed steps of Madame Gervaisais' advance and retreat along the road to conversion are well done, but even this position is hard to sustain because, as Ricatte admits himself, "Madame Gervaisais does not have in her the stuff of a true novelistic character" (430). The attempt to provide her with an authentic past is frankly fraudulent. We are told that she is a philosopher, a painter, and has real talent, but never does the reader get any glimpse of her accomplishments. She has no permanent relationship with other adults that attach her to a milieu. Mindless, she floats disembodied through pages rich with description and barren of action. Further, her turning against her own child seems unconvincing and thereby weakens what is of value in the psychological study. The satire of the clergy is heavy, and in fact the sense of heaviness is pervasive, in part because there is so little dialogue. This absence of human give and take may be due only to the fact that she never has anyone to talk to but is more probably due to Jules's failing creative powers. For some incredible reason Alphonse Daudet found the novel to be the Goncourts' best, but it leaves today's reader with a feeling of distaste and disappointment.

V   *Jules's Death*

Perhaps the Goncourts felt this same sense of failure. The entry in their *Journal* following the completion of the novel begins: "Disgust, profound disgust. The irony of things."[27] When in January they corrected proof, they wrote that their life was full of busy trivia "in the midst of mutual malaise . . . one tormented by perpetual migraine headaches, the other by nausea." Even going out socially seemed empty of meaning. At Princess Mathilde's, "always the same transients, the same comings and goings, the same handshakes . . . the same impression of indifference, of dessication. . . . Beneath the banal chit-chat, useless words."[28]

Their mood became even gloomier because of the friction that developed between them and the distinguished critic, Sainte-Beuve (who was to die that very year). They had hoped that he was enough of a friend to give them a good review of their book, but in private conversation with the authors Sainte-Beuve had been grouchy and harsh. The Goncourts concluded that he would probably tear their book apart and said so one evening at the Princess's. When this tidbit got back to the great critic, he used this comment as an excuse not to review the book at all. By the end of March, the *Journal* records: "A time for rain, a time for dreaming. Days dozing . . . when one isn't even sure one exists."[29] Problems with noise increased even more, and in May life in Paris was a "Hell," so in June they left to take the waters at Royat. But illness was making travel increasingly difficult. "Intestinal complaint. All night long I writhed on the train like a cut earthworm."[30] And having arrived, they experienced "days when in the emptiness, the *ennui*, the cares of the eternally long day, one tries to put the cruel present to sleep in a kind of somnolence—more days buried in the black silence of thought."

July was the saddest month of their lives: "We leave here, this accursed country, these waters of suffering, these hotels of noise, these dining rooms forever filling up with new groups of fools." Suddenly at the end of September, the *Journal* ceases to record entries for that year, except for a few notes covering two pages. What energy they had left was spent in working on a biography of their old friend Gavarni. New Year's Day greeted them with solitude and suffering. The *Journal* picks up again briefly until January 19, 1870, when Jules made his last entry. Months later Edmond picked up his pen again to tell of his brother's last days. In March, Edmond noted that Jules was losing his speech, the letters "r" and "c" were too much for him, then the fine mind began to dissolve. Jules could no longer spell, and he frequently could not recognize objects. He developed a mania, which was to read Chateaubriand's *Mémoires d'Outre-Tombe (Posthumous Memoirs)*, but even this great work could not halt the disintegration. In May Jules partially lost the power of speech, and his days were spent gazing bleakly out into space. He finally died on June 20, 1870. Edmond wrote with relief: "He is dying, he has just died. God be praised!" and added: "The Magny dinners were founded by Gavarni, Sainte-Beuve and us. Gavarni is dead, Sainte-Beuve is dead. My brother is dead; will death be content with just half of us, or will it take me soon as well? I am ready."

A unique literary collaboration had drawn to its painful end. It had produced some works of value, but could Edmond continue alone? True, he was only forty-eight years old, but he was tired, and it seemed as if he and Jules were Siamese twins, neither of whom could live without the other. Perhaps in a sense it was fortunate for Edmond that the Franco-Prussian War broke out that summer. It gave the grief-stricken survivor something with which to fill what would have been very empty, lonely days.

CHAPTER 6

Edmond Alone: La Fille Elisa

I *War, Siege, and the Commune*

THE summer of 1870 was somber for Edmond. "I am sad, broken, obliterated," he wrote on July 20, and he had to struggle to continue the *Journal* that he and Jules had kept for so many years. But the man of letters in him asserted itself enough for him to keep on, if only to chronicle his fatigue and inertia. His despondency increased as he began dreaming of his brother, somehow both alive and dead in his nightmares (July 27). However, private misfortune was swept away by public events, for during the summer France embarked upon the disastrous war that was to topple the Empire. As Edmond walked the streets of the capital in a effort to shake off his personal grief, he found himself observing the changes in the city that had been brought on by the outbreak of hostilities. Little by little he began recording in his *Journal* these vignettes of a nation at war. At first the entries were brief and related only to the narrator himself, as he witnessed the early enthusiasm of his fellow citizens: "At the stock market, from top to bottom, all you can see are bare heads, hats waving in the air, and in everyone's mouth a roaring Marseillaise, whose waves of sound drown out the noise on the floor of the stock market inside. Never have I been the witness of such enthusiasm. One walks among men pale with emotion, children hopping around, women acting intoxicated." But Edmond resisted the temptation to use the scene as a springboard for an abstract essay. His moral judgment is delivered through the concrete details of the scene: he encounters a man so hallucinated by joy that he tries to point out to Edmond a non-existent victory bulletin on a wall (August 6). The symbolism is obvious.

With the beginning of the military reverses the change in the scenes became pronounced and began to appeal to that esthetic sense in him which relished the spectacle of disintegration: "I find at the St. Lazare Railroad station a group of some twenty Zouaves, the remnants of a battalion that had gone into action under MacMahon. Nothing is so beautiful, nothing has so much style, nothing is so sculptured, so pictorial as these exhausted refugees from a battle. They bear on themselves a weariness comparable to no other weariness and their uniforms are worn, faded, as if they had drunk the sun and rain of years" (August 23). Little by little Edmond was becoming a chronicler of the war and the seige of Paris. There was no lofty detachment about his reporting, for Edmond was an ardent nationalist, and he could become more than a little annoyed at the Olympian views of his acquaintance Ernest Renan, the great historian, who seemed to be above national prejudices and spoke in the name of all humanity. Edmond suffered keenly at the presence of German troops on French soil and, like everyone else, had conclusions to draw. He blamed the failures of the French on the lack of discipline in the working class and saw this slackness as having been fostered by the moral laxity of the Empire, but he avoided the simplistic polemics of those who blamed it all on the emperor's private excesses. But despite his opinion, he preferred to concentrate on the description of the physical aspects of the city, an attitude in accord with the esthetics of Realism, and one which incidentally permitted him to avoid propaganda and maintain some objectivity. Just as his technique was excellent in describing the confusion of bric-a-brac in Coriolis' studio, so it served well for painting Paris under siege:

All along Suchet Boulevard, along the interior fortification road, the joyous animation and grandiose movement of the National Defense forces. All along the road they are making fascines, gabions, filling sacks with earth, hollowing out powder magazines and oil storage drums in the trenches. Up on the pavement former customs-office barracks, the echoing muffled fall of canon balls, tumbling off trucks. Up above on the platform, canon practice by civilians; down below gun drill by the National Guard. One sees passing by silent bands of workers, the blue, black and white shirts of the Mobile Guards; and in the kind of green canal of the railway, the rapid flash of trains, only the upper part of which are visible, trains red with soldiers' trousers, stripes, epaulettes, and hats of this military population. (September 11)

Edmond's success in capturing the kaleidoscopic scene led him to write more and more extended descriptions, and by September 19, when the Germans completed the encirclement of the capital,

Edmond had clearly undertaken the task of responsible reporting of the total picture, in an effort to penetrate the illusions of war, to lay bare its deadly reality. He was acutely conscious of the illusions of his compatriots, and he sensed irony even in the weather: "Nature seems to enjoy the contrast that novelists like for their intimate catastrophes. Never has the décor of September been so laughing, never has the sky been so pure, the weather so beautiful" (September 26) as the disaster loomed. This illusion was reflected in Edmond's opinion by the political "changes" that occurred when the Republic was declared. On September 21, on the anniversary of the proclamation of the First Republic, there was a parade in honor of liberty. Edmond was furious at what he considered playacting, convinced that the Republic gave no freedom and merely shifted power from the hands of one set of adventurers to another. Illusion was even more obviously a factor in the press, for to sell their newspapers, sensational news items were cynically fabricated. "Journalists of the present hour are robbing the public," declared Edmond on October 16 in scornful anger. He was disgusted by euphemistic military bulletins that labeled retreats as "offensive reconnaissances" (October 20) and by invention of nonexistent victories. Even when reporting was honest, the constant illusory hope quickly destroyed by reality was a terrible and exhausting experience. Even Edmond's own self-centered world at times seemed unimportant: "I look at this house full of books, *objets d'art*, of engravings, prints, which will create holes in the history of the French School if it all burns, and these things which were loves . . . before, I don't have the energetic desire to save" (August 25). He noted the fact that he had lost interest in buying old historical pamphlets.[1] At times he admitted his selfishness openly: "I desire peace keenly, I desire very selfishly that no shell fall on my house and bibelots" (November 11). On January 16, 1871, he worried again about their destruction, but the caricature of Edmond whose only concern in the war was his collection of objets d'art is unjust. As a patriot he railed at the defeatists and grieved over the surrender. He had a truly lofty goal of being a responsible journalist, even a modern historian, who would tell the Truth about the war. He chronicled all the daily miseries and examples of cowardice, the lack of leadership and discipline, the omnipresent concern for food as stocks dwindled. His conclusion is categorical: "Let prosperity not try to tell future generations about the heroism of the Parisian in 1870.

His entire heroism consisted in putting rancid butter on his beans and eating horsemeat instead of beef—and this last without really being aware of it, as the Parisian has little discernment about what he eats" (November 12).

The end of the siege brought relief to Paris and to Edmond. The Germans were "correct," and Edmond could write on January 24, 1871: "I was seized this morning by a desire to write *La Fille Elisa*, this book which we were to write, he and I, after *Madame Gervaisais*. I wrote a few lines on a piece of paper. It will perhaps become the first chapter." But the Commune made him postpone literary creation. In the following months Edmond underwent all the agonies of that upheaval, including bombardment of his own home in Auteuil, and he even witnessed the death of *communards* at a barricade. Never had his descriptions been more graphic, and never had they communicated so well an immediacy of reality as can be seen for instance, in a detail of the entry for May 23, 1871: "The National Guardsman, with angry violent gestures, as if shouting to someone off stage, indicates by signs that he wants to pick up the dead man. The bullets continue to make leaves fall on the two men. Then the Guardsman, whose face I can see is red with anger, throws his rifle on his shoulder, butt in the air and walks towards the rifle shots, insults on his tongue. Suddenly I see him stop, put out his hand to his forehead, for a second lean his hand and forehead against a tree, then half turn around and fall on his back, arms outspread." In summary, the year 1870-71 was rich in tragic experience for Edmond with the death of Jules, war, seige, famine and surrender, followed by the civil war. It is conceivable that this reporting, with its heavily historical and sociological concerns, had an influence on *La Fille Elisa*, which too is heavily sociological, so much so that at times it seems to move out of the realm of fiction altogether and become journalism.

II   La Fille Elisa. *Sources*

The origins of *La Fille Elisa* go back to 1862, and a notebook full of jottings makes clear that Edmond and Jules collaborated closely in their research with the intent of writing it after they had completed *Madame Gervaisais*.[2] This year, 1862, was significant for their novel in three ways. First, the reader will recall that in 1862, when the Goncourts' servant Rose died, it was Jules's mis-

tress Maria, a midwife, who revealed to the Goncourts Rose's hidden
life. This glimpse into the lower social depths not only inspired
Germinie Lacerteux but also provided part of the impetus for *La
Fille Elisa*. The *Journal* contains some information that goes back as
far as April, 1858, but in May, 1862, Maria's lifestory was set down
in detail. The story of her life shows the link between midwifery and
prostitution, which is a typical pattern for a girl who is seduced,
made pregnant, and then abandoned both by her lover and by her
family and forced out into the streets. When as a consequence she
becomes pregnant again and needs an abortion, she gets to know the
clandestine milieu in which midwives live. Because midwives know
prostitutes well, the Goncourts decided in their novel on prostitution to make the heroine a midwife's daughter.

The second event of 1862 that gave them another part of their
projected novel was a chance visit on October 28 to a woman's
prison located in Clermont d'Oise. Fortunately for posterity, the
Goncourts wrote in detail of their visit in their *Journal*. Limitations
of space preclude our citing this fascinating account in its entirety—
there are more than six pages—but in brief, after describing the
general exterior, Edmond and Jules tell of their talk with the
director, a self-satisfied, jovial chap whose gaiety so contrasted with
his surroundings that the Goncourts were chilled. Then they were
given a guided tour of the establishment. They concluded their
record with this key paragraph: "The horrible things about these
rooms, the horror in this scene and in this prison is the torture of
this penitentiary system, this philanthropic and moral torture
which has gone beyond the excesses of physical torture, but which
makes no one cry out, makes no one indignant . . . because there is
no blood, no cries; it is a 'dry' torture and a torture which, instead
of crippling the body, mutilates the soul and kills the mind: it
results only in creating madwomen, many madwomen every year,
said the official [*sous-préfet*] smiling. This torture is silence." The
Goncourts were appalled at the system: "Tear out a person's tongue
rather than remove his speech," they declared, for as men of letters
they knew that words are life itself. They rejected the claims of the
prison officials that the Auburn system (of American origin)
improved the inmates' morality. Hypocrisy, bitterness, and lesbian-
ism were rampant. As Ricatte comments: "Never perhaps had the
shock of a scene that they had observed hit them so utterly, never
had they had the feeling of finding themselves before a reality that

must not be forgotten or minimized."[3] The prison must therefore
become a part of their future novel. Therefore their heroine must
commit a crime, a prostitute's crime.

This grim thinking was reinforced by the third relevant event
of 1862. The Goncourts read Victor Hugo's *Les Misérables*, which
had just been published, and commented after their visit to Clermont: "Thinking about Clermont, I reflect on how little imagination provides . . . in comparison with truth. See *Les Misérables*
of Victor Hugo."[4] The two brothers sensed the necessity of com-
bating what they felt to be the literary falsehoods of fiction dealing
with prostitution that were popular at that time, and it is true that
Dumas' *La Dame aux camélias* (1852) and Hugo's sentimental
treatment of Fantine in *Les Misérables* do not communicate a sense
of social reality, inasmuch as such nasty problems as disease, crime,
aging, and degradation were usually circumvented by a convenient
literary death for the heroine.

For all these reasons the Goncourts were eager to be faithful to
social reality, and therefore in 1863 they spent days looking through
the *Gazette des Tribunaux* for an actual crime that would fit the
needs for their future novel. In the course of their research the
wider social implications of the world of prostitution became
increasingly evident to them. The notebook shows their interest
in the role that wealthy bankers play in the life of courtesans, the
problem of disease, the police, and prison, but much of this background material never appeared in the final version of the novel
(as it would in Zola's *Nana*). When Edmond began to write, he
avoided—as he and Jules always had—the tendency to present
a large fresco and concentrated rather on the personal immediacy
of one individual's plight. Further, he was now convinced that
while he would use a prostitute for his protagonist, his main purpose was to attack the Auburn prison system. Finally, fearful lest
the novel be suppressed by government censorship, he therefore
eliminated more deeply searching preoccupations that might
embarrass people in high places.[5]

The polemical nature of *La Fille Elisa* is stressed in a ringing
preface in which he proclaims, in an explicit parallel to the preface
of *Germinie Lacerteux,* his mission as a "doctor, scholar, and historian." Once again he demands that the novel be something other
than a frivolous pastime. He warns that his portrayal of prostitution
will not be titillating, as is the case with so many novels, and above

and beyond the world of vice is his concern with the penal system.
"My ambition," he writes, "is to lead people to study works on
prison madness, to do research on the number of imbeciles who are
today in the prisons of Clermont, Montpellier, Cadillac, Doullens,
Rennes, and Auberive . . . and finally to be able to touch the
emotions of our legislators."

As Ricatte has pointed out, this didactic intent justifies a critic's
judging the novel on its accuracy of reportage on the prison system;
he goes on to show that the presentation of the Auburn system is
unfair and partial. Edmond's sources in penology are unreliable,
and some good ones are overlooked. Ricatte's conclusion is that the
indignation of the novelist was so strong that he used sources to
buttress his emotions, without much regard for fact. Further, if we
move now to literary considerations. Edmond often included
material that seems irrelevant. For instance, a form used by
prisoners for writing letters is reproduced exactly, as are routine
details of the dining-hall menu. These minutiae may in the
tradition of journalism show life as it was in the prison, but they
make the reader conscious of an occasional loss of artistic harmony
in which all elements serve an imaginative goal. Nevertheless,
although at times the work seems as much reporting as it does fiction, it is still a novel and should be judged as such, and therefore
we should expect setting, characters, plot, and ideas to fuse into an
over-all unity supported by the general structure.

The opening chapter is reminiscent of that of *Soeur Philomène*,
where the initial scene in which Elisa is condemned to death for
murder, sets the tone of the whole novel. As the jury deliberates
night is falling in a prefiguration of death. The prisoner is absent,
but nobody cares much, for we are in a world where procedures,
events, and even objects seem to have priority over people, as is
shown by the opening paragraph: "As night was falling, in the
yellowish dusk of the end of a December day, amid the fearsome
shadows of the Court of Assises that was blending into the darkness,
while some invisible clock was striking the hour, out of the midst
of the judges with blurred faces and red robes, there had just come
from the toothless mouth of the presiding magistrate, the impartial
Summing-Up." Not only the toothless mouth and the red robes
seem to have an existence of their own. There are also the state's
exhibits—a soldier's trousers and bloody shirt, a knife that attracts
the spectators' eyes to it, and the prisoner's hat hanging with limp

ribbons near the door to a detention room. In fact, the objects dominate the scene to such an extent that they seem to live, while the people there seem reduced to objects: "In the light of the candelabras, one could see mindless groping gestures, hands buttoning coats, without any thought behind the act" (p.16).

Into this grim scene the prisoner is led to hear her sentence. Although full of life when she bounds across the threshold into the courtroom, under the impact of the death sentence she seems to lose her human qualities, and her gestures are reduced to the instinctive reflexes of her nervous system: "At the words of 'head cut off,' the condemned woman, throwing herself forward in a final lunge, her mouth clogged with words, with her nervous fingers began to knead her hat which soon became a rag. . . . Suddenly she brought it up to her face . . . blew her nose in the shapeless thing . . . and without saying a word, fell back on the bench, holding her neck in her two hands, and clutching it mechanically like hands trying to hold a wobbly hand on its shoulders" (18). This first chapter, then, is symbolic as well as real, serving as an overture to the entire work. Just as Elisa appears here first as being full of life but then is quickly reduced to inarticulateness, so too in her life does she first appear as an individual with a range of possibilities open to her, only to be destroyed as a person, reduced at the end to a mute, tortured, dehumanized number in prison, where she finally dies. She is the eternal victim, Edmond seems to be saying, who must wait dumbly until the moment comes when society strikes her down.

After this prologue, the story reverts to Elisa's youth to show her character in its early formative stages. By 1876—the year in which Zola's *L'Assommoir* began appearing in serialized form—it was a commonplace to assume that some mixture of heredity and environment produced human personality, and true to the new vogue of Realistic and Naturalistic literature, Edmond started with the girl's mother and the impact of environment on *her* character: "An abominable life was that of little Elisa with her mother. The effort of pulling out children [*tirer des enfants*], the daily climb of fifty storeys, going out day and night in all kinds of weather, no sleep, keeping vigil in unheated houses, the care and exhaustion of an overtaxed existence, everything exasperated the midwife's temperament, kept her in that grumbling irritation of people who work at hellish jobs" (23). The effect of this grueling existence is to make the exhausted woman a poor mother and thus to prepare the daughter's desire to leave home.

Elisa's character was partly formed by attacks of typhoid fever, which left her with a psycho-physiological weakness (28). She had fits of violent temper and could easily be swept into an irrational mood; then feverish activity would be followed by weeks of torpor (31). Thus, both the uncertainty of the milieu plus the instability of her nervous system meant that she would be ill-suited for the steadiness and responsibility that a midwife must have to ply her demanding trade. She was, therefore, prepared to drift into the world of prostitution and would find it easy to detach herself impulsively from her mother and to turn to the oldest profession. What else could she do, knowing no other trade and being too lazy to learn one?

This excellent explanation of her nature makes the reader believe in her as an individualized character, but once Elisa is installed in a provincial bordello, the novel shifts its focus from the individual to the group. This shift fits the intention of the author, for as he wrote in his *Journal*: "The principal feature of the girl who has fallen into a life of prostitution is her personality. She is no longer a person, no longer someone, but only a member of the herd. Consciousness of the self and the sense of owning oneself fade out to the point that in big houses, the girls eat out of each others' plates with their fingers."[6] To the individualistic Goncourts, this loss of personality is the worst thing that can befall either a person or a society. Sabatier correctly stresses their idea that "Assemblies, companies, societies can always do less than one man. All great things in thought are created by an individual effort, just as are all great creations of the will."[7] This personal concern was matched by the fact that this milieu was really little studied in fiction (We remember that Zola's *Nana* was not to appear until 1880), and Edmond wished to make a sociological study of the prostitute simply because it had not been done. Chapter 13 is actually nothing but an essay contrasting houses and whores in Paris and in the provinces. At first Elisa seems different from the other girls because of her Parisian background, but she soon loses this distinctiveness and blends in with the others. Once more she has been shaped by her milieu. This shaping can take some unexpected forms. For instance, the very grossness of her occupation leads the average prostitute to try to compensate for it, to create a dream life in which virtue and the ideal predominate. Edmond observed that among the girls who could read, they devoured cheap romances: "The more simplistic the action is, the more untrue to life the plot is, the harder it is to swallow, the greater the defects in art and truth, and the less the characters are real, the more romance has a hold on this kind of woman" (71). The unchaste woman, far from being attracted by pornography, revels in stories of devotion and chastity—the further from the truth the better.

Edmond's commentary is of course also a personal one, for we know that he and Jules had always considered the average piece of fiction a tissue of lies, and as historians and seekers after truth they had often heaped scorn upon it and said that their own *romans* were consciously trying to avoid the plots and the unrealities of typical fiction. But even Edmond had to admit his bafflement, as he intruded into the text to soliloquize: "The novel! who will explain its miracle? The title warns us that we are going to read a lie, and after a few pages, the lying print fools us if we were reading a book 'where it really happened.' We give our interest, our emotion, our tenderness, a tear sometimes to a human story that we know never took place. And if *we* are deceived, how could the uncultivated working-class woman avoid being taken in?" Edmond realized further that "out of the confusion . . . of things she reads, the woman of the lower class is imperiously, involuntarily led to substitute for her own personality the imaginary personality of fiction, to cast off her own miserable and prosaic self and to enter forcibly into the poetic and fictional skin of the heroine: a true incarnation which continues long after reading the book" (73). Edmond noted that at this time—the Second Empire— romances about the Greek War of Independence were particularly numerous and offered an exquisite combination of war, captives, and escapes, all in an exotic setting. Elisa, reading this trash, lived in an "awakened dream" of noble actions. Then, bringing to bear his long years of observation of illusion and reality, Edmond tested the heroine to see if this bad literature could have enough impact to actually create an authentic new personality.

One day a traveling salesman shows up at the establishment and claims that he is a secret agent of the "Marianne" society (a Republican group dedicated to the overthrow of the Second Empire). His tales of derring-do stir Elisa's imagination, and she concludes that he is "in flesh and blood the hero conjured up by her dreams" (82). She leaves the bordello, which by now bores her, to follow the man. The disillusionment is swift, for he is actually a government stool pigeon, and she really does not love him but loves the illusory idea that she thought he represented. When she learns the truth, the fragility of the personality created by bad literature is made clear, and in strong reaction she becomes hostile to all men (88), a dangerous attitude in one of her calling.

After this disaster, she floats from house to house, always seeking "something better" and, of course, never finding it (100). The constant mobility, the excesses of the flesh, a life in cloistered houses, fatigue, worries over the debts which trap her in the system —all accumulate to overwhelm her with discouragement. She finds herself on earth but outside the pale of the law and without recourse against injustice. Worse yet, she has an obscure awareness that she is no longer a person who can control her destiny, that she is not even a person at all but rather a creature at the bottom of the social ladder, buffeted by the whims of others. Her mind becomes less clear, her body less individualized through exploitation.

At this moment in her career she enters a bordello near the Military Academy in Paris. Edmond had visited establishments of this kind and could give an authentic flavor to this milieu. He describes the girls at the ending of the evening in the hothouse atmosphere of the *maison close*: "You could see the women with sleep-filled movements . . .wrapping themselves in tartans, old shawls, any old rag, looking for the benches surrounded by the least amount of spittle. They lay down on them, inert, broken, spilling out like packets of shabby laundry. . . . Immediately they fell asleep and, from time to time, were awakened by their own snoring. Disturbed for a moment from their troubled dreams, they lifted themselves up on an elbow and looked stupidly about" (115). Dehumanization and degradation can hardly be carried further than in this chilling description.

As the human psyche must assert itself when possible, Elisa reacts against her stultifying environment by trying to recreate herself as an authentic person. She is limited by her job and her temperament, by the result of society's formation and her entire life. Hence, no prince charming can ride up on horseback. But she does have the good fortune to acquire a genuine suitor: an ignorant Breton draftee named Jules. Chapter 29 is an essay which gives a shrewd analysis of the relationship between a soldier and a prostitute. While the military success of the Second Empire prior to the catastrophe of 1870 gave the French uniform some glamour in the eyes of the prostitute, the main attraction for her was that soldiers, usually of peasant origin, had not been corrupted by city vice and remained more frank and open—if at times brutal—in their dealings with a whore. Often, dazzled by the "glamour" of the bordello, they fell genuinely, if awkwardly in love. In short, "for the soldier the whore remains a woman" (135). The relationship is based on illusion to some extent, of course. The glamour of the house is false and the love is for sale, but even so, "something of the ideal falsity of dreams is attached to these girls and makes them attractive to these men" (139). The result is that real—if precarious—opportunities for love can arise.

So with Elisa and Jules. Each time he comes he brings her a cheap bouquet of flowers. In her eyes the past is obliterated and her profession is forgotten, for he has appealed to that strong sense of the ideal that, paradoxically, her profession has formed in her. She falls madly in love (Chap. 33), wanting it to be ideal, even feeling that "the contact of her skin would sully him." But hostility to the male is still part of her personality. One day, when she is feeling most keenly the sense of a chaste ideal, Jules tries to make love to her and in a sense assaults her. Suddenly everything comes together: the early instabilities, the waywardness, the horror of the male, the unreasoning emotionalism: she stabs and kills him in a frenetic act of which she is not even conscious. Far from being an absurd gesture , a Gidian *acte gratuit*, it is an entirely explainable, although not justifiable, act. The thoughtful reader will perceive the truth thanks to Edmond's careful preparation of this moment, but the jury of Elisa's "peers" cannot see the truth. Their only solution is to condemn her to death, Edmond's way of showing illusion at work in the judicial system of our society.

In order to show the evils of Clermont, Edmond permits Elisa's sentence to be commuted to life imprisonment at "Noirlieu" (Black place) a visible transposition of Clermont (Clear, bright mountain). Under the Auburn regime of silence, Elisa disintegrates. It is evident that Edmond drew upon his own painful recollections of Jules's final collapse, when Elisa discovers that "objects appeared diffused to her and no longer revealed their general shape, while at the same time she could absorb an infinite number of tiny details in her mind" (170). Then she comes to the point where she has a kind of "mental somnolence that kept her from seeing, feeling, suffering; . . . accomplishing acts in a stupid absence from herself" (174). This disintegration is presented as taking place in an environment where the penal system claims to be morally uplifting, but under the ironic sign "God sees me," the prisoners invent any number of dodges to avoid detection of their thoughts. The hypocrisy that the Goncourts observed at Clermont is an effort to preserve an authentic inner world that the system cannot touch. But even this inner world crumbles. Bit by bit, Elisa loses her sanctuary of the mind, and just before her death, she reverts at the age of forty to the age of four, imagining in a last illusion that she is a little girl again playing in sunny fields. Then the ultimate reality of death strikes, and she is no more.

La Fille Elisa impresses today's reader as being most visibly a novel of social protest. While it is true that out of fear of censorship, Edmond left unexplored the world of pimps and rich roués, his narrative still makes clear society's failures. Edmond and Jules may have been hostile to the *political* demands of the poor and had no love for their company, but they knew social injustice when they saw it and were outraged. Fosca claims that without Jules, the social preachment is heavier because the style is heavier and less sprightly.[8] This is no doubt true, but rather than a defect, it adds to the sense of oppression that pervades the novel. Despite this heaviness, when the novel was published by Charpentier in January, 1887, it sold 10,000 copies in a few days when normally the Goncourts' fiction was barely noticed by the general public. The sales were due, as is so often the case, to the furor in the newspapers over its "illicit" subject matter.

But even if we ignore the sensationalism that surrounded *La Fille Elisa* and consider the reaction of serious writers and friends of Edmond, there was less than total enthusiasm, Alphonse Daudet declared the book beautiful in a letter to Edmond, but Princess Mathilde said to the unhappy author: "How you do write things that are not at all like you. It's abominable, abominable," and she would not even listen to Edmond's defense.[9] Edmond no doubt attributed this *ad hominem* criticism to the stupidity of women, but even Flaubert, who believed in Art like the Goncourts, was disappointed. Comparing it to Zola's *L'Assommoir* in a letter to Madame Roger des Genettes, he asked: "Do you know *La Femme Elisa?* It is brief and anemic, and *L'Assommoir* seems like a masterpiece in comparison; because in Zola's long pages, one finds real power and an undeniable temperment."[10]

Flaubert's harsh criticism does point to certain weaknesses in the novel. For instance, the structure is based on an alternation of present reality and flashbacks in a manner that at times becomes mechanical, and Elisa's fellow prostitutes are often just listed and do not participate in the development of the narrative or of the heroine's psychology. But Flaubert's reservations are due primarily to the fact that, unlike Balzac, himself, and Zola, the Goncourts did not show individuals and society in their complex interaction, nor paint tableaux that had continuity in time, nor create secondary characters with a life of their own. The aristocratic Goncourts instinctively shied away from crowds and were never happier than when the action moved inside and unfolded behind closed doors. Progressive isolation seems the normal pattern for their fiction, whether in *Renée Mauperin, Germinie Lacerteux,* or *Madame Gervaisais,* with the consequence that the number of secondary characters is almost automatically reduced. This refusal to paint a broad literary canvas is at times a weakness in the Goncourts' fiction, but here it is fully justified. In a novel that examines the progressive dehumanization of an individual, detachment and increasing solitude are entirely appropriate.

CHAPTER 7

The Brothers Reunited:
Les Frères Zemganno

E DMOND wrote in his *Journal* on December 27, 1876: "Now
that my book on *La Fille Elisa* is almost finished, there is suddenly beginning to appear and to take on a vague outline in my
mind the novel with which I dream of bidding farewell to the imagination. I would like to create two clowns, two brothers who love
each other as my brother and I did. . . . In it [there would be] many
details of the life of the younger, and the brotherly feelings of older,
with some fatherly ones mixed in. The older—strength; the younger
—grace, with something of the poetic nature that one can find in
the lower class, and which would find its outlet in the whimsy that
the English clown brings to his act."[1] The *Journal* continues with
notations which would become the essence of the plot. But a year
and a half later we find him still in the process of thinking out the
details of the opening scene,[2] and by October of that year, the work
still lay ahead of him, as he mused: "It seems to me that I must
get to my novel on the two clowns, for I find myself at this moment
with my mind in a vague and fluid state which suits this work which
lies a bit outside absolute reality."[3] By December he was finally at
work: "In this novel of *Les Frères Bendigo* [as it was at first en-
titled], there are several chapters that I'm composing with the portrait of my brother before me. It seems to bring my work good
luck."[4] In the preface to the novel written on March 23, 1879, Edmond explained: "This time I have created an imaginative dream
mixed in with memories." In short, the current of inspiration came
in part from an imaginative interpretation of his own life, in part
from the world of the circus. But how did he happen to choose the
circus for the setting of the novel? It seems like an odd milieu for
refined esthetes.

First of all, as Edmond explained in the preface, while novels
like their own *Germinie Lacerteux* and Zola's *L'Assommoir* had

119

fixed in the public consciousness the idea that Naturalism dealt almost by definition with the lower segments of society, Edmond looked forward to the day when a writer of talent would make these pitiless analyses of people in the more educated strata of society, with their subtler and more sensitive types. Then and only then, he reasoned, would Realism prove its definitive triumph over the moribund schools of the past. He saw that task as a difficult one, however, for the educated person's subtler nervous system is harder to portray than the animallike peasant and worker. He and Jules were to have been—thanks to their own exquisite sensibilities—the ones to accomplish this broadening of the modern novel, but with his brother's death, Edmond had abandoned the task, which he felt to be beyond him. Unwilling to explore the social heights alone, and having resolved to stop writing about the lower depths, he compromised by combining the two, choosing the world of the circus, humble in origin and in class yet aristocratic in temperament.

The Goncourts were habitués of the circus. As early as November 21, 1859, the *Journal* notes: "We go to only one theater. All the others bore and irritate us. The theater to which we go is the circus. There we see men and women jumpers, clowns, leapers through paper hoops who do their profession and their duty. . . . Their talent is a fact. We see then, these men and women, risking their bones in the air to get a few 'Bravos!' with a deep feeling in our entrails, with something curiously savage in us, and, at the same time, with a sense of liking them and pitying them, as if those machines were of our own race, and that we all of us . . . historians, philosophers, clowns and poets, leap heroically for the idiot public."[5] They repeated this idea of the joint supremacy of men whose life is of the body and those whose life is of the mind in 1865: "The two finest conquests that man has made over himself are the somersault and philosophy."[6] And they seemed certain that "man" did not mean all mankind, for they went on to say: "As a matter of fact, do you know that the somersault is the greatest superiority of men over women?" Frankly, one has difficulty even understanding their prejudice on this score when they could see with their own eyes so many superb female gymnasts and high-wire artists. On September 18, 1867, they recorded the pleasure they experienced at these feats of physical prowess: "We are assiduous in our attendance at the Athletic Arena, at this spectacle . . . which really gives your nervous system a working over."[7]

But *Les Frères Zemganno* was to be far more than the description of a specialized milieu. Edmond reminded his readers in the preface that they "complain of the harsh emotions that contemporary writers give them with all their brutal realism; they hardly suspect that those who create this reality suffer from it more than the readers, and that sometimes they remain nervously sick for several weeks after the time that the book has been so laboriously and painfully brought into existence." This confession reinforces what is obvious anyway: the novel transposes into fictional form the relationship of Edmond and Jules de Goncourt.

I *Autobiography Transposed*

The two fictional brothers of the novel, Gianni and Nello Bescapé, are born of a gypsy mother into a small-time wandering circus troupe whose director is their father. Gianni, like Edmond, is much older than Nello, and when their mother dies she puts her two sons' hands together, as Mme de Goncourt had done with her sons. When the father dies a few years later, Gianni must act as father as well as brother to Nello. The emotional alliances of the Bescapé family are also copied from real life. The mother had preferred the younger, more handsome son, and Gianni struggled to accept this preference just as Edmond had bowed to a similar ranking of himself and Jules: "Gianni, who had a loving nature under a cold exterior, suffered from this unequal sharing of affection, but without having this preference for Nello create in him any jealousy against his brother. He recognized that he was not handsome and was rather melancholy by nature. He spoke little. . . . Even his expression of filial love was clumsy, whereas his brother was a beautiful and winning youth" (66).

Early in childhood, Nello learns to be an acrobat under the guidance of his older brother, who works with a safety rope attached between them (thus suggesting a kind of umbilical cord, for the two are truly inseparable). Eventually the two become almost one, like Edmond and Jules (99). In addition to the close professional bond, they develop identical tastes: "The two brothers not only loved each other, but were linked by mysterious . . . psychic attachments . . . like that of twins, although of different ages and of opposite character. Their first instinctive reactions were always identical. They liked and disliked similarly, and when they went out in the evening, they returned feeling the same things about the people they had

seen" (172). Their existence as professionals was a chaste one, without women, for they believed that "their strength could be con-
served only by depriving themselves of Bacchus and Venus, a
tradition that descended directly from the wrestlers and gymnasts
of antiquity" (180). At the height of their triumphant career, when
performing a new and dangerous trick before a packed house in
Paris, their act is sabotaged by a fellow trouper, an American equestrienne, who hates Nello. The younger brother breaks his legs in a
fall and can never perform again. Like Jules de Goncourt, he disintegrates as a personality and even complains of the noise around
him (264). The novel does not close with Nello's death but with their
having to abandon their life's dream. Henceforth they will be circus
violinists sitting on their chairs, an end as tragic for them as death
itself.

There are deeper elements to this story than those facts given
above, and Edmond chose as his technique for arriving at more
fundamental truths the interplay of illusion and reality. Some years
after the publication of *Les Frères Zemganno* Edmond told of his
excitement at seeing a play featuring a clown, Paul Margueritte's
Pierrot, assassin de sa femme. He was intrigued by the "Mobility of
the mask . . . and the succession of painful expressions that he makes
pass across his neurotic flesh."[8] The careful reader will recall that the
theater has appeared as a motif in much of the fiction that we have
already discussed in the preceding chapters. In *En 18 . .* there is a
brief scene of an actor playing the role of a drunkard. In *Charles
Demailly* Marthe is an actress. In *Renée Mauperin* there is play
within the story, as in Shakespeare's *Hamlet*, and Madame Bourjot
learns the truth that her lover Henri is planning to marry her
daughter. The posturing of people at a masked ball is important in
Henriette Maréchal and in *Manette Salomon*. In the latter novel,
too, the Goncourts make good use of a monkey to explore Anatole's
character, and in a sense the monkey is a living mask, a clown figure.
In each case there is illusion but at the same time, paradoxically,
a deep truth is revealed. Illusion, while a barrier to understanding,
becomes in the last analysis a means to understanding.

In *Les Frères Zemganno* illusion and reality are present from the
opening chapter. The itinerant Bescapé troupe arrives at a cross-
roads in their rickety wagons and stops for the night. The scene
seems to capture only the humdrum details of these simple people.
We watch each of the travelers going about his assigned duty. One

of the women, for instance, is involved in preparing supper, "silent, touching nothing, and giving orders almost as is done in a pantomime." But as the group acts out the drama of man's essential needs of food, fire, and sleep in the face of nightfall (a traditional death symbol made explicit here as "the death throes of the life of light"), the lack of dialogue and stylized ritual gestures suggest that the surface activity is an illusion that hides a deeper reality. The scene is symbolic of mankind's efforts to assert its life force in the face of death and of the uncertainty of the meaning of existence. The Goncourts stress the "uncertainty as to the appearance of things," as if to underline the ambiguity of life and to show that in the interplay of illusion and reality it is sometimes difficult to be certain which of the two is the deeper truth.

When we move to the world of the circus we find that its spectacle, too, unfolds at night, and that illusion is the dominant theme. "There are, in the kingdom of flashy tinsel, painted faces, charming and bizarre effects of light. At times there plays across the needlework of a tight-rope artist's costume a cascade of gold that creates a tapestry of fireworks. . . . On the face of a clown surrounded by light, the white flour shows starkly the clean outlines, the regularity, the almost abrupt silhouette of a stone face" (152). The action, too, highlights the illusions of this specialized stage. In those days it was common for pantomine sketches to be acted out by the gymnast-clowns. One example given in the book tells of a girl stuffed in a bag, magically escaping through an apparently seamless bottom—minus all her outer clothing. Nello is particularly sensitive to this odd milieu and calls it a "bizarre lie" (156).

But as we have said, the "falsehoods" of illusion are often "truer" than reality. Hallucinatory pantomime can reveal deep psychological truth just as in earlier novels nightmares and dreams offered clues to the central personality of the characters (e.g., Soeur Philomène). In *Les Frères Zemganno* Edmond is able—thanks to the possibilities of the milieu—to transfer the nightmare from dream to concrete reality in the form of a pantomime before a real audience. In this drama the most profound truth, not only about the characters, but about the author, is laid bare. Gianni and Nello act out in the circus ring this living nightmare. The plot is simple: In the semidarkness of the ring Gianni lies asleep. From a cloud a blue mist Nello appears suddenly as an imp from the underworld, symbol of the diabolical in Gianni's nightmare. He awakens the sleeper by his brooding presence and then takes refuge behind a tree and begins to rasp out discordant notes on a violin, provoking Gianni to chase him. The pursuit, full of dazzling acrobatics, ends in a wrestling match, "whose apparent furious struggles were in fact graceful embracing and disengaging" (143). The imp is overthrown and, astonished, humbles himself like a slave before his master. Then Gianni takes out a violin and plays sweet music, which exorcises all the evil from the other. Thus delivered, Nello joins his brother in playing a pastoral idyll in perfect harmony. Within the reality of the novel, the scene expresses something of the life of the two acrobats who do enjoy playing the violin together, whose union is so real that it may be called love, and whose perfect relationship is destroyed at the end of the novel when they must end as "racleurs de violons"—sawers on the violin—their harmony broken. But as we said above, this pantomime is also a revelation concerning the Goncourt brothers.

Edmond not infrequently had nightmares and two that he recounted from his later years are illuminating. In the first, he imagined himself ill and a woman arriving in mourning; from her gown a priest leaps like a jack-in-the-box and forces him on his sickbed to sign a marriage contract.[9] The other nightmare which Edmond says frequently returns to haunt him, tells of his getting lost in a provincial city, asking for a hotel, but the hotel turns out to be a bordello. The owner of the establishment has apparently performed in the circus. Edmond tries to get back to some party he has just left, but without success, and he meets a frightening hunchback. Finally an intimate friend goes off with a woman, abandoning him, and he awakens in complete solitude.[10] The fear of women is of course obvious in these accounts, and its presence in nightmares suggests its deep-seated nature. If we look again at the pantomime, remembering that Nello has "something feminine" about him, "white skin . . . a small mouth" (129), and that a woman was even jealous that Nello was a friend of her lover because he had a "woman's mouth" (183), it is not difficult to sense the homose.ual overtones of the circus pantomime.[11] There are other clues as well. When crippled, Nello begs his brother not take another partner, and the two are described as married (99), because in their twin somersaults they become one, a comment all the more telling when we recall the comment that the somersault proves the superiority of men over women.

Before a complete understanding of the pantomime can be

reached, however, a fuller explanation of the role of music and the violins is needed. In one of the earliers pantomimes in their fiction, a burlesque impromptu in *Charles Demailly*, there appears the following bit of dialogue:

"—Good quicksilver, please tell us now what a poet is."

"—All right, Bourgeois. It's a man who puts a ladder against a star, and climbs while playing the violin." (60)

The playing of a violin is obviously viewed as a symbol for the creation of anything artistic, and the ladder to the star represents the quest of the ideal. But why choose the violin as a symbol of Art? An early *Journal* entry describes the décor of a church with "saints swooning on the cross with the movements of hysterical violinists."[12] More personally, "the hands of one of us seem like our talent itself: a nervous hand, a hand of a sick man or of a violinist."[13] Any high-strung person is referred to as "vibrating," and the effect of a high-pitched note could drive the Goncourts out of their minds. For this reason Edmond was particularly intrigued by the Margueritte play mentioned above, because as a background for the clown's twitching features, "the young musician Vidal has composed a score quite appropriate to the 'nervosity' [*nervosisme*] of the thing." The violinist is also the poet. If the music is beautiful, it symbolizes the ideal artistic achievement; if grating, it tells of evil, of fragmentation, and more specifically portrays the nervous *fin de siècle* art and decadent man. The Goncourts found the image the most suitable manner of expressing their own high-strung artistic selves.

Now to interpret the pantomime further: Gianni is at peace until Nello arrives, for the younger awakens the elder to his presence as sexual desire. The chase represents both a positive and a negative force: to unite with the other, for he is desirable, and to destroy him because homosexuality is taboo. Because Gianni-Edmond accepts traditional moral codes, the tempter is portrayed as coming from hell, and the discord of the violin symbolizes the evil involved. When Gianni catches Nello the ambiguity of desire-rejection is maintained with a struggle of opposition on the one hand and the embracing and disengaging on the other. When Nello is overthrown, his prostrate form again suggests the woman's role. But the relationship cannot as yet be viable and beautiful, for the aspect that is evil must be dealt with. Its exorcism is accomplished through music, the symbol of all art. The message then emerges: as novelistic collaborators, their latent incestuous homosexuality was transformed into a relationship that both could genuinely, deeply, consider a human perfection. The Goncourts were indeed fortunate to have been able to solve their problem as well as they did.

But Edmond was not content to limit his use of illusion and reality to this level, important as we have shown it to be. Beyond interrelationship lies the problem of individual identity. Nello discovers that he must face the question: Which is he, real man or real artist? When made up in grease paint, disguised by his performer's costume, suddenly

a new life, a life different from the one he led in the morning, an odd life, began to flow in his veins. Oh! it was not for the clown a feeling of metamorphosis. . . but still there took place in Nello small abnormal phenomena . . . his voice was no longer the same as his normal one . . . and in his gestures . . . he could feel his limbs twist into odd shapes. Even more, when alone, he was pushed into making the gestures of a somnambulist and a madman . . . gestures over which he had no control. One day he found himself projecting finger silhouettes against the wall . . . as if his body obeyed hypnotic impulses. (155)

Progressively, the outer clown absorbs the inner man, "as in the midst of a disappearance of reality all around him . . . the clown got to the point of no longer being able to see anything but the reflection of his white face in the mirrors." This special state of being had "great sweetness" for Nello, who spends considerable time in this trancelike other existence. But Edmond seems to draw no clear conclusion and is content to leave the question of illusion more real than reality at the level of an unresolved problem. The literature of the twentieth century—one thinks especially of Pirandello—would later take up the question where Edmond let it drop.

II Critique of Western Man

Edmond was more interested in Gianni, his other self; and through the older brother, Edmond undertook to explore one of the biggest problems of Western man himself: that is, precisely those qualities that make him Western man. To understand this point, the reader must return to the opening pages of the novel and the presentation of Gianni's Gypsy mother, who is non-Western in origin and psychology. Steucha Roudak, forced into marriage with the European Thomas Bescapé, is not assimilated into Western culture but retains the non-Western desire of accommodating herself to nature rather than forcing nature to yield to herself. The incident in which she encases a hedgehog in wet clay and then roasts it alive in the fire is not only startling, it marks her as coming from a culture alien to our own. Only her body lives in France; her mind refuses Western values. Even her God is the vague Prester John of the East, "whose relationship with his subjects takes place through the voice of nature" (34). Her love for her child Nello (an infant when the novel opens) is portrayed as instinctual, and when she dies it is without the metaphysical anguish of Westerners. She resembles an animal curling up under a bush to get through its last moments. Even the "Western" members of the troupe become like her, thanks to their eternal wanderings through the country. They develop the soft numbness of "dreamy isolation, the hidden, contained intoxication of primitive man continually in contact with nature" (78). This Gypsy attitude is continued in Nello who prefers to let Gianni do all the planning and thinking in their life.

In contrast to Nello, Gianni seems eager to overcome the limitations of nature. He trains his body so that it can seem to defy natural law, and his mind also is active. He has his heart set on going to Paris (symbol of the center of Western culture [37]). The others of the troupe, Rabastens the strongman and the clown Agapit Clochegru, are too subhuman to have this ambition (38). Gianni, with a highly developed Western *libido sciendi*, even thinks in terms of defying the law of gravity. When Nello asks him what he is up to, he answers: "I'm looking for something" (91). The something is the new acrobatic stunt. Gianni explains: "There is within me a passion, a sickness to find something that will make us famous" (179). Nello warns that the price of reaching for the stars may well cost more than it is really worth, a prediction that eventually comes true, but Gianni persists, for that in his nature: to dream, not vacuously, but with his intellect trying to impose his will on his culture and, beyond that, on nature. His goal, perilous to the point of self-destruction, would be incomprehensible to his Gypsy mother, but the main antagonism does not come from this quarter, as his mother dies early in the novel. His Western idealism finds its most deadly opposition in a perverted form of that very Western striving. We refer to the villainess, Miss Tompkins, the American equestrienne. We have seen that on the sexual level woman is for the Goncourts the enemy of man. On the social level, the American is the enemy of what is good in European culture. This fear of "Americanization" of Western Europe was as commonplace at this time even as now, and Miss Tompkins is a typical example of the caricature of the barbarous American. The essential distinction between the two Occidentals is that Gianni works to express that which is noblest in humanity, whereas Miss Tompkins, fabulously rich uses her financial power diabolically, that is, to subvert human efforts and to dehumanize others through the power of the dollar. Like Gianni she has the essence of the Western soul: "to create the impossible, the superhuman, things forbidden by nature and by God," but "with the brutality of desire of the American race which has come to possess money" (179). She is rich enough to be able to purchase a Viennese mansion and by use of technology create an artificial storm within the edifice! The function of this detail is to show that man can replace nature itself, an idea incidentally that prefigures Huysmans' À Rebours (Against the Grain), the masterpiece of French decadent literature that was to appear in 1884.

To the Goncourts, Art was one of the noblest of human expressions. Therefore, Miss Tompkins both as woman and as American has a deep-seated desire to profane it. "When the word got around in the newspapers that there was an extremely expensive painting . . . for sale, good or bad, exquisite or mediocre, she arrived in a cab, took from her wallet the agreed on sum, and went off with the canvas on the roof of the cab, without giving her name. And in her room . . . nailed in boxes, all wrapped up, [were] all her purchases which she never looked at again" (191). Worst of all, her money could destroy people: "she would buy for a thousand francs from the owner of a restaurant near the circus, the dismissal of a waiter whom she objected to—one never knew why or over what incident—because he looked like a 'barometer salesman'" (193).

When the feminine Nello spurns the advances of this masculine, cigarette-smoking equestrienne she never hesitates. She pays someone to substitute a wooden prop for a canvas one when Gianni and Nello perform their new acrobatic stunt in public for the first time, and this substitution brings about Nello's serious injury and the disastrous end to their personal and professional harmony. Léon Hennique in his postface to the novel claimed that he knew the

woman who was the prototype for Miss Tompkins, an Italian named
Lucia Morgantini (282). But Miss Tompkins is intended to be
larger than life, representing the dangerous, diabolical power of
Western man which offsets his noblest creations. Edmond very
wisely avoided concluding that one side was the "truer" vision but
instead limited himself to presenting the dual nature of Western
man, in which horror and grandeur are equally mixed.

Coexisting with the psychological and metaphysical aspects of the
novel is the fine portrayal of the world of the circus. As habitués
of the popular Winter Circus and Summer Circus, the Goncourts
had acquired a good knowledge of the life of the performers, such
as the famous Hanlon Lees brothers. Edmond explains the different
styles of English and French schools of acrobatics and clowning and
goes so far as to include the entire contract which Gianni and Nello
sign with the Paris circus. The sociological value of this document
is considerable, in that the contract shows the complete absence of
protection to the performer in case of accident, the power of
management to annul the contract after six months, and other
evidence which shows how unprotected the circus performer was in
a pre-union era. Léon Hennique, evoking his own memories, concludes that all the circus types portrayed by Edmond—the strongman, the clown, the high-wire artist, and so on—were absolutely
typical. It is not only a matter of the exteriors: physique, dress, and
living arrangements, but also of psychology. When the troupe
gathers in a tavern, Edmond notes their special walk visible under
their street clothes, their games of dominoes played without a word
uttered, for these men express themselves through their muscles
(158-159), and their taciturnity is due also, Edmond informs us,
to their despondency over advancing age when the muscles will no
longer obey the commands. Indeed some of them have already had
a serious accident, and although they have "fully" recovered, they
are called *les démolis* (the wrecks). They have lost their sublime
confidence and must now make an extra effort to perform well. The
strain of this effort is marked upon their faces and in their unspoken attitudes. To this general background is added professional
detail about the intricacies of acrobatics. For example, as Gianni
tries to develop a higher leap, we are reminded of its anatomical
complexity: "For a leap to be successful, you must achieve a bend-
ing of the leg and thigh, and of the torso against the thigh, all on
a foot braced on the ground. Then in the shortening of the body,

in this lowering of the center of gravity . . . you need a quick release of the extensor muscles. . ." (200). The over-all impressions is one of accuracy and truth.

Les Frères Zemganno, one may conclude, is no mean achievement. Sociologically accurate in its description of a milieu, and believable, with one exception,[14] in its presentation of the psychology of circus performers, rich in its inner exploration of the love between two men, and in its wider exploration of the double-edged nature of Western man, it stands as the last great work of fiction to come from the Goncourts. True, there was but one brother left to write, but as Paul Guth has remarked: "When they were two, they seemed to be only one; now that they are one, they seem to be two."[15] Les Frères Zemganno deserves to be better known.

CHAPTER 8

La Faustin *and the Later Years*

IN the twilight of his career, Edmond turned once again to the world of the theater. In 1856 he and Jules had put together a biographical volume entitled *Les Actrices*, and in 1890 Edmond reverted to biography with *Mademoiselle Clairon*, which was followed in 1893 by *La Guimard*. In that latter year, Edmond's brief one-act farce, entitled *A bas le progrès (Down with Progress)*, was played by André Antoine at the Menus Plaîsirs theater. This bit of froth (written in 1891) was dismissed as valueless by the newspapers, although it makes pleasant enough reading today. As further evidence of Edmond's interest in the theater, he was having his novels adapted to the stage, as we saw above in Chapter 4 with *Germinie Lacerteux*. It is not surprising therefore, that Edmond's last full novel *La Faustin* has for its subject the life of an actress.

I La Faustin

As was the normal pattern for the brothers' fiction, the idea for the novel had been long in coming to fruition. In the *Journal* for July, 1862, they wrote: "There is deep within me, buried, ready, but not yet having an outlet, an ambition: the ambition to take a woman who is worth it, to be impenetrable to her while seeming to give myself up to her, to *break* her, as they said in the eighteenth century. Not that I love evil or suffering, but it strikes me as being a flattering superiority, to keep one's mask in love, to appear to be but a child, and to be her master. A great actress, for example, like Rachel, I would have liked to possess her and remain a mystery to her, to seize her, study her, to penetrate her, and never to reveal myself."[1] The puerile sadism of this entry is hardly attractive, although it does testify to an aspect of the Goncourts' psychology that cannot be ignored. But the passage in its serious desire to understand the nature of an actress's character is an initial step toward exploring the interrelationship between an actor as a man and the role that he creates before an audience. The idea was touched on in the following years. In a sense Elisa was by profession a woman wearing an actor's mask, feigning love for money, and we have seen that Edmond pondered the interaction of the two aspects of Nello—the man and the clown—in *Les Frères Zemganno*. Now the problem was to move to center stage, and it was clear that, as far back as 1862, they foresaw that the tragedienne Rachel would provide them with the basis for their study.

We can guess why Edmond kept this early idea of using the famous actress. First of all, unlike the great Sarah Bernhardt, with whom Rachel had much in common, she was dead, and a suit for libel was less likely. There was also the fact that the two brothers had come to know Rachel's sisters after the actress's death from tuberculosis in 1858: "There was there a sister to Rachel, Lia Félix, a miniature of her sister . . . [who] has slept with nearly everybody."[2] The next month, another entry: "The women are Lia, her sister Dinah, who has the small snake-like head of a Faustine, with velvet black eyes and her wavy hair in stiff small curls which are the sign of dark little passions in women."[3] But the sisters of Rachel were vulgar people whose main contribution was to enable Edmond to reach into the world of the theater in order to learn the details of the life of their more distinguished sister.

Elizabeth-Rachel Félix, born in 1821, was the daughter of an itinerant Jewish peddler. As a child she was obliged literally to sing for her supper on street corners. Like a heroine in a fairy tale, she was discovered by a man who could sense talent, who removed her from her milieu and developed her as a singer. But her true vocation was acting and by the age of seventeen she was already a star of the Paris stage. The high point of her career may have been her performance in the titular role of Racine's *Phèdre* in 1843. It can even be argued that much of the success of the brief Classical revival in France at that time was due to her own incandescent acting, for Rachel was superb in the plays of Corneille and Racine, although she was only average in "modern" roles.

The Goncourts were attracted not only by her talent but also by her background. They had that same sense of curiosity about *le peuple* here as in *Germinie Lacerteux*. They also saw in the oddities of her behavior some of their own decadent feelings. The *Journal* tells the following anecdote about Rachel: "One evening on leaving the Délassements [a comic theater] she absolutely insisted on going

to the Café du Géant, and when told it was absolutely impossible,
she insisted on drinking . . . out on the boulevard . . . a jaded palate,
a weary and unsatisfied woman, whose vulgar tastes from time to
time returned, tempting her with the hope of a new ecstasy. . . .
Beautiful as the satiety of a Roman empress."[4] This last phrase
suggests the origins of the novel's title, *La Faustin*, for Fausta (the
original title contemplated by Edmond) and Faustina evoke brilliant, talented, and corrupt Roman empresses.

In the years following Rachel's death, the Goncourts dined with
Lia and were to be seen in her salon.[5] But many years passed before
Edmond announced in the *Journal* (October, 1877) that he was
caught up by his novel on the "Actresses" to the point that his pulse
raced and he developed a slight fever.[6] Not until August 27, 1880,
did the vision become complete: "Today in the middle of a bad
headache, La Faustin suddenly erupted in my brain. . . ." Soon he
was hard at work. "Every day, I'm happy like a child who has been
made slightly tipsy. I don't feel my body, and my brain seems like
a gas. This flight into the world of La Faustin delights me because
it proves that my imaginative machine is still working." At this time
he begged Dinah Félix to tell him how her sister used to rehearse.[7]
She could not tell him, but as she was herself an actress, brought
him to her own rehearsals to see how things went. By April, 1881, he
was reading his completed manuscript to Zola, Daudet, the pub-
lisher Charpentier, and a group of "young realists." To judge from
the *Journal*, the novel was not very well received: "I'm astonished.
The chapters documented with the keenest perception of humanity
don't seem to go over. On the other hand, the chapters that I scorn
somewhat, the chapters of pure imagination, really grip this small
audience. The Greek Athanassiadis [a minor character] is taken by
Zola as being a person sketched from real life."[8] Edmond was never
a good critic of his own work. Today's reader has the same impression as did Zola. Art and life are not the same things. But despite
his friends' mixed reaction, Edmond was undaunted, and the novel
appeared in book form in 1882.

The plot of the novel is simple enough. La Faustin, as she calls
herself, is a famous actress of the Comédie Française of the 1840's
who has, like Rachel, some rather disreputable sisters and a never-
ending stream of admirers. She gets the chance to play Racine's
Phèdre, and we see her at work both at rehearsal and during a performance. These chapters that explore the tensions of an actress

preparing her role are excellent. She performs wonderfully, but one wise old critic lets her know his disappointment, blaming her less than perfect performance on her bourgeois life shared with an intelligent, steady, but unexciting broker. In order to play at her greatest, he says, she must experience a passion resembling that of Phèdre herself. The arrival of an extraordinary Englishman, Lord Annandale, whom she still secretly loves after an earlier affair with him in Scotland, gives her an opportunity. Their liaison becomes the talk of Paris, and her performance of *Phèdre*, for "him alone," is sublime, as if there were perfect interaction between her private being and her professional role, each enriching the other to create a moment of sublimity. But this superhuman achievement cannot possibly have duration. Soon her lover becomes jealous of her life in the theater. Trying to save their love, she resigns from the Comédie Française and for a time is happy with Lord Annandale in the provinces. But she discovers that her whole being now includes professional acting, and she longs for the Parisian stage.

Meanwhile one George Selwyn, an old friend of her lover, has turned up. It appears that he is a diabolical pederast who had led Lord Annandale astray in earlier years, before the latter's love for La Faustin saved him. Then suddenly Lord Annandale falls ill and dies of an obscure disease, one which gives to the face of the dying man a ghastly rictus, making him look like a "satanic caricature" (265). Unfortunately, La Faustin sees this expression and against her will, her training as an actress comes to the fore and compels her to imitate the rictus with her own features. As she does so the dying man has a last moment of lucidity, realizes what she is doing, and, horrified by the comprehension that she can never cease being an actress, that she probably was never more than an actress, that she is all exterior mask, that she cannot love, he orders her out of the house.

The appearance of Selwyn, although of no great value to the development of the plot, is of importance in terms of the author's psychology, for it shows Edmond's urge to treat overtly the theme of pederasty, which in *Les Frères Zemganno* was sublimated. There is no approval of homosexuality in *La Faustin*; rather one senses it as something attractive but evil. But more basic to the point of the novel is the elaboration of the illusion-versus-reality theme, where illusion (the life of the stage) becomes a person's reality, as Lord Annandale realized in his dying moments. As one might expect,

Edmond prepared the theme systematically. The opening chapter[9] shows the actress on a beach at the seashore in the gathering darkness at nightfall, and the chiaroscuro permits Edmond to mingle illusion and a sense of dream with reality, much as was done in the opening chapters of *Soeur Philomène* and *Les Frères Zemganno*, whose opening scenes also take place in semidarkness. The second chapter, set in Paris, is more social, showing the pretention of the salon of La Faustin's sisters who—because of their ostentation—cannot hide their basic vulgarity. When the scene moves to the rehearsals of *Phèdre*, at first the novel emphasizes the difference between the actors as persons and as role players. They come on stage in street clothing with their usual human concerns, making a jarring contrast to the lines that they are speaking. Then the actors become more engrossed in their parts until harmony is created because they have become their roles for the moment and have discarded the reality of their personal lives. This is especially true for the heroine, who obtains that brief moment of fusion mentioned above. There is, then, another aspect of Edmond's view of the illusion-reality problem. At the same time that he could consider the impact of one upon the other, he also saw that if they can become one they cannot become one permanently. If through the magic of love or genius they can be fused as in the heroine's performance of Racine's play, it is only for a fleeting moment, before the cruel realization that man is hopelessly separated from an illusory perfection sets in.

The first rather cool reaction of Edmond's friends was typical of the novel's general reception, despite its excellent re-creation of the world of the theater and the profundity of the treatment of the basic theme. Although the "Naturalistic" authors like Zola loyally rallied around and praised this "human document" and the "verve of the style," one senses their lack of enthusiasm. Perhaps one should not entirely trust men like Barbey d'Aurevilly and Ferdinand Brunetière, for they detested the new school of writers, but Jules Vallès—himself a Naturalist—was shocked at the immorality of the novel (although he did not really explain why).[10] Actually, one serious flaw in *La Faustin* is the "hero," Lord Annandale, who is a grotesque caricature of the English aristocrat. For instance, when inspecting a new Parisian home in which to live with his Juliette (La Faustin), he utters only two words on the whole inspection trip: "bird" and "bath." Edmond apparently saw these two subjects as the only things that could wrench an English lord out of total taciturnity. Equally unsatisfactory is the final *agonie sardonique* of a disease which, conveniently left unexplained, is far too literary a device to inspire belief. While Edmond declared it true to life ("vraisemblable"), he also had to admit that it was an invention of his imagination.[11] Clearly its purpose was not medical but moral, suggesting, in the satanic appearance that the rictus gives to Lord Annandale's face, the evil of the British character. His coldness and his suppressed homosexuality (which the French of that epoch called "the English vice") give an almost allegorical quality to the hero, and allegory is out of place in a novel that tries to re-create the reality of France in the mid-nineteenth century. The rictus is no more convincing on the realistic plane than in Victor Hugo's *L'Homme qui rit* (1868), in which the hero has had a perpetual laugh carved into his face by means of an operation. Finally, the deathbed scene reveals a complete failure on the part of Edmond to grasp the psychology of either a woman in love or a great actress, neither of whom would feel "compelled" to imitate the dying grimace of a beloved person.

II Chérie

Chérie, Edmond's last effort at fiction, was announced in the preface to *La Faustin*. In it he made an extraordinary plea: "Just as a historian gathers bits of paper about women of the past, why should not today's novelist (who is basically only a historian for those who have no history) use the same method. . . .?" After announcing that he wished to write a novel "which will supply a psychological and physiological study of a girl who is raised in the hot-house atmosphere of a capital city," he states that he has discovered that his documentation, in books written by men about women, lacks the feminine touch. So he calls upon his feminine public to provide him with intimate psychological details of the life of a girl from early childhood to maturity. But the idea for his study was, once again, the result of years of meditation. In 1865 after seeing little girls at play, the two brothers wrote: "How interesting it would be for a rich man to take one of these little creatures at this age, a little girl, that is a woman minus the hypocrisy, the native Eve, to follow her, to study her, to analyze in her the phenomenon of love as something tender and transparent."[12] The basic idea began to take shape in 1878, thanks to Mademoiselle Marie Abbatucci, a lady-in-waiting of Princess Mathilde. Edmond knew Mlle Abbatucci well enough in

1874 so that rumors began to fly that Edmond might marry her. In September, 1878, Edmond confessed to his *Journal* that he found her attractive and that, if he were younger, he "might be tempted to marry her in order to write about women and young unmarried girls of the era novels such as are not and never will be written."[13] One evening in 1878 Mlle Abbatucci began to tell him about her life as a girl, and during the years 1878-80 the *Journal* records several bits of feminine psychology that would one day find their place in *Chérie*. Mlle Abbatucci was not, however, Edmond's only source. Another friend, Pauline Zeller, sent him her diary of the time when she was sixteen years old, and the diary appears, along with the confessions of Mlle Abbatucci in *Chérie*, which was published in 1884.

A literary rivalry was the source of one part of *Chérie*. Edmond had been increasingly jealous of Emile Zola's success and was particularly irritated by the younger author's excursions into high society, about which he knew little. Edmond, we remember, had felt that to analyze this sophisticated world was an extremely difficult task and that without Jules he did not feel able to undertake it. In *La Curée (The Spoils)*, published in 1872, Zola had described the fashionable dressmaker of the Second Empire, Worth, and discussed women's fashions in some detail. Edmond felt that Zola knew nothing about the matter and went out of his way in *Chérie* to outdo his rival. Edmond's sense of nuance of color and cut stood him in good stead, and his treatment of the subject is without question more sophisticated than Zola's. Another point of rivalry, although this time unintentional, came about because Edmond, wishing to show that he did not lack "realistic" vigor, told in detail of Chérie's first menstruation. When Zola published *La Joie de vivre (Zest for Life)*, which includes a similar scene, before *Chérie* appeared, Edmond accused Zola of plagiarism, for Edmond had read chapters of his fiction to his assembled friends while Zola was still working on his novel. The implication was that having stolen the idea, Zola rushed to have his novel published first. But Zola was able to remind Edmond that the chapter concerning the onset of menstruation was *not* one that Edmond had read aloud, and therefore the similarity was coincidental.

In spite of all Edmond's documentation, heightened sensitivities, and realistic energy, *Chérie* is a very anemic work compared to *La Curée*. Many of Edmond's most stubborn faults remain. He uses the same mechanical device to introduce secondary characters that he and Jules had used in *Charles Demailly*: a simple listing in one chapter of all of Chérie's friends; only at the end of the work do any of these other young women reappear in the narrative. As a result, Chérie floats detached from life despite Edmond's effort to integrate her into the Parisian scene in the 1860's. Another flaw is the absurd intellectual premise on which the "novel" (for lack of a better word) is constructed. Chérie Haudancourt, daughter of a cabinet minister, is brought up by her grandfather who spoils her badly. When she reaches the age to be married she is too fussy, and suitors are put off by her slim dowry and luxurious tastes. Thus by the time she is twenty-one she is still single. Then comes the surprise. We are asked to believe that ovulation without fecundation in a Parisian woman of high-strung temperament often leads to madness and death, which is indeed Chérie's fate. The date of her death, incidentally, is given as June 20, 1870—the date of Jules de Goncourt's death. What this choice meant in Edmond's mind we can only guess at. Finally, the "novel" lacks even a simple plot. Edmond was not only aware of this absence, he was proud of it: "I am trying in *The Marshal's Granddaughter* [an alternate title] something that no longer resembles a novel. The lack of a plot isn't enough any more. I would like the context, the form to be different, I would like the book to have the characteristics of a person's memoirs, written by another. Decidedly," muses Edmond in a brief excursion into esthetic theory, "this word *roman* no longer names the type of book that we write. I would like to find a new label, which I keep looking for but can't find, which would have the word *Histoires* [a word which here combines "Histories" and "Stories"] with some *ad hoc* modifier, but that's the hitch—this adjective. . . . No, we need a single word to debaptize the nineteenth century novel."[14] He reinforces this attitude expressed in the *Journal* with a comment in the preface to *Chérie* that there are still too many plot incidents to suit him. Actually, the fiction gives in chronological sequence a series of vignettes. Some of these are delightful, like the opening chapter which tells with great charm of an elegant dinner party given in honor of Chérie's ninth birthday. As little girls sometimes will, they act very grown up and formal. But when they've had a taste of champagne, then childish exuberance mixes with regal bearing. A sample: "The mischievous little girl in the Scottish dress is making a series of marvelous faces which are judged by Chérie unworthy of the solemnity of the place, and which she stops with a sharp: 'Where does Mademoiselle think she is?' " Many of the vignettes are successful, and yet many seem quite pointless, for not only do they fail to constitute a plot, they do not even fit in with the stated purpose of the biography, to wit, that modern society is destructive of women, who become so warped by the artificial life they lead that they cannot love, marry and procreate in natural rhythm. *Chérie* is, despite some delightful fresh evocations of childhood life, profoundly pessimistic. And when he had finished writing it Edmond was equally somber: "I am suffering for the first time, perhaps, since my brother's death, from finding myself alone. When I was writing novels, when I was creating characters, my creations kept me company, supplied me with a circle of friends, and peopled my solitude."[15] Edmond de Goncourt still had years to live and much to write but was no longer driven by the need to create fictional worlds.

III   *The Académie Goncourt*

Instead, he turned his efforts to perpetuating his reputation. This preoccupation had always been there, but in 1884 he was sixty-two years old, and he felt with increasing exasperation that the younger generation did not appreciate him as it should; it did not see him as the master who had renovated modern literature. The *Journal* of his declining years records his pathetic gratitude at any letter of praise that came from any budding writer, and his anguish at the indifference of the press to the many achievements of himself and Jules. It was due in part to this growing feeling of being forgotten that he had been planning to found an academy in their name. As early as June, 1882, the public had gotten wind that some project was under consideration. Ernest d'Hervilly revealed in *Le Bien Public* the essence of the plan: there would be a board of ten members (each to receive an annual stipend of 6,000 francs) who would select a writer each year for a prize of 5,000 francs. Actually, the initial idea went back to July, 1867, prior to Jules's death. The *Journal* muses: "It is rather strange that no legacy has been left to an author. . . ." André Billy suggests, reasonably enough, that this initial hint took on concrete form during the discussions of the Magny dinners.[16] Finally, a will dated July 14, 1874, contained the names of future directors: Flaubert, Saint-Victor, Veuillot, Banville, Barbey d'Aurevilly, Fromentin, Chennevières, Zola, Daudet, and Claudel. These names represented much of the best literary talent of the day, representa-

tive of new directions in literature, particularly Realism, and
Edmond also chose people who would *not* be elected to the
Académie Française, or who, if elected, would refuse membership.
The best authors of that era had nothing but scorn for the official
French Academy. With the passage of time, the list of directors was
inevitably modified. Several died, others fell from Edmond's favor,
including Zola who had stood for election to the Académie Française
in 1890. But despite difficulties, the Académie Goncourt was constituted after Edmond's death in 1896. It opened its doors in 1903
and began the annual giving of a prize the same year, and it still
today tries to encourage and honor new novelistic talent, following
Edmond's injunction that "our idea has been to assist the development of budding talents."[17]

IV   The "Grenier" and Last Years

There was both idealism and vanity in this scheme of the Académie Goncourt. Edmond did indeed want to help the young writers, but it must be confessed that he really wished to help only those
who acknowledged him as master. He dismissed the new poets of his
day as dirty Bohemians, never recognizing in Baudelaire, Verlaine,
and Rimbaud talent that surpassed his own. His desire to perpetuate
his name and influence led him to found not only this Académie
Goncourt but also his famous "Grenier," or Attic. At his home in
Auteuil, Edmond had for many years entertained on Sunday his
closest friends, Flaubert, Daudet, the Russian Turgenev, and Emile
Zola. When the former died in 1880, the meetings were abandoned,
but after some years Daudet and Zola suggested that he open his
home to his literary friends once more. The upper floor was re-
modeled, and the Grenier was inaugurated in 1885. At first many
came, but Edmond was not a sparkling host, and it was often said
that when Daudet was not present, boredom reigned. What was
discussed at these meetings was, unfortunately, not usually transcribed in the *Journal*. That it was always literary, we know, for once
when Guy de Maupassant tried to talk business, he was quickly
squelched. Despite the less than total enthusiasm, a coterie was
formed from which the future directors of the Académie Goncourt
were recruited. It was from the Grenier also that there arose difficulty between Edmond and Emile Zola. In 1887, Zola's powerful
novel, *La Terre (The Land)*, was appearing in serial form in the
Gil Blas, and its crudity prompted five young men—the older

Rosny, Paul Bonnetain, Paul Margueritte, Lucien Descaves, and Gustave Guiches—to write a manifesto against it. This attack on Zola and his naturalism was published in *Le Figaro* on August 18, 1887. The five signatories were indeed presumptuous to have written such a moralizing tract, for they themselves had published fiction dealing with such indelicate topics as prostitution and masturbation. With time, it became evident that Zola was more helped than harmed by the resultant publicity. The main question was whether Edmond and Alphonse Daudet had put the younger men up to this action. Zola apparently believed so, at least at first. Edmond was most probably innocent, but Zola could not be blamed for his suspicions, as four of the five signatories were members of the Grenier and the fifth, Guiches, became one shortly thereafter. Zola knew also that Edmond did not care much for his work, an opinion borne out by perusal of the *Journal*, for the entries show frequent criticism, especially of Zola's poorer efforts, but no mention at all of a masterpiece like *Germinal* (1885). The split between the two was real for a time, and although it was papered over, they were never close friends after that episode. In the 1890's, Zola drifted away from his former friends, while Edmond and Daudet, closer in taste and temperament, renewed a friendship that lasted until death. Edmond dined frequently with the Daudets at Champrosay, and the *Journal* records the many illnesses and sorrows of their final years. Edmond continued to work, although not very systematically, publishing slim volumes on the Japanese artists Hokusai and Utamaro. As if conscious that Edmond might not live much longer, the world of letters organized a banquet in his honor in 1895, upon the occasion of his being named an officer of the Legion of Honor. On July 16, 1896, he died of pulmonary congestion that developed into pneumonia, and he was buried in the cemetery at Montmartre on July 20. Zola, who could appreciate his worth whatever their literary and personal differences may have been, gave a moving speech in his memory. Other important figures associated with the schools of Realism and Naturalism soon followed him to the grave. Daudet died in 1897 and Zola in 1902. Edmond's death seemed to have signaled the end of a literary movement and the close of an entire century.

CHAPTER 9

Conclusion

I N the race for literary immortality, the Goncourts started with a heavy handicap, for it seems as if they almost deliberately set about to alienate their future judges, the literary critics of the twentieth century. They scorned women, Jews, the working class, the bourgeoisie, and foreigners, relying with vague trust on future artists and men of letters to keep their memory alive. How much they sensed that more might be needed can be deduced from their founding of the Académie Goncourt, which would preserve their name. And it is indeed true that modern critics have been revolted by their anti-Semitism, misogyny, and smug aristocratic attitudes. Abandoned by those whom they had hoped would be their future allies, they did not even have, like Victor Hugo, a huge popular reading class that was cheerfully prepared to ignore the critics' displeasure, for their fiction could never have the appeal òf *Les Misérables*. By their own admission they lived a self-centered life, and they further alienated the average reader-critic by their unwillingness to cloak their views with conventional morality. They wrote trenchantly about this once in their *Journal*, commenting on contemporary hypocrisy: "I am looking for a man who makes no pretense of caring for his fellow man, who founds no hospitals, who is uninterested in the poor . . . a man who does not sacrifice himself for his brothers, who is not dedicated to journalism, to politics, to speeches in favor of the wretched, the poor, the suffering . . . a man who doesn't have to be good, who isn't interested in progress, an egoist, yes, by God! I'd love to find one, to see one, true, brutal, cynical and sincere."[1] While we have seen that there is a more compassionate side to Edmond and Jules than the above suggests, the outburst does point to a selfish aspect of their natures. These men who came to dinner spent their lives in other people's drawing rooms, rushing home late each night to distill their nasty little remarks in a diary so venomous at times that even the complimentary entries offended people when it was published. Even a critic willing to be sympathetic has a hard time in warming up to them.

Inevitably, personal hostility of the critics has influenced their criticism. The Goncourts often spoke of their interest in others, of their desire to penetrate beneath the surface of real or fictional beings, to explore the recesses of the human heart, but the critics are eager not to believe them. Auerbach obviously delights in being able to show that there is condescension in their attitude toward the working class in *Germinie Lacerteux*,[2] and Jean-Pierre Richard is equally glad to demonstrate that their descriptive technique can do nothing more than play over a hard exterior, never penetrating below the surface.[3] This inability to do more than to show the exterior is presented as meaning that the Goncourts viewed people as they did their bibelots: amusing objects to look at from the heights of their own superiority. But true as is the above criticism, it fails to take into account the sense of human compassion of which Jules and Edmond were at times capable. One should never forget the ringing prefaces to *Germinie Lacerteux* and *La Fille Elisa* in which they pleaded for an understanding of the working class and protested against unjust penal conditions. And on occasion in their *Journal*, in the midst of all the gossiping one can find a brief compassionate sketch of human suffering that they have observed. To judge these two as men is difficult, for ample evidence exists on both sides of the ledger. But while biography properly deals with these human judgments, the literary critic must forgo the pleasure of praise or denunciation of the authors and limit himself to their work.

A dispassionate study of their works might profitably begin with Edmond's own assessment of their literary career. In the preface to *Chérie* (1884), Edmond recalled that one day in early 1870, just a few months before Jules died, the younger collaborator had cried out suddenly:

I don't care . . . people can deny as much as they want, they will have to recognize some day that we wrote *Germinie Lacerteux* and that it is the prototype for all that has been done since under the name of realism, of naturalism, etc. That's one item.

Now, through our writings, our talking about it, through our purchases . . . who imposed the taste for eighteenth century art and literature? Who would dare say that we weren't the ones? That's item two.

Finally, the description of a Paris salon full of bits of Japanese art, published in our first novel . . . which appeared in 1851 (and show me the lovers of Japanese art of *that* period), and the acquisition of bronzes and lacquers during those years . . . and the discovery in 1860 of the first Japanese album to be known in Paris . . . . and the pages given over to things Japanese in *Manette Salomon*, in *Idées et sensations*, don't all these make of us the first propagators of this art . . . one which, without anyone's being aware of it, is in the process of revolutionizing Western culture? That makes three.[4]

In the same preface Edmond added a fourth item: "A novelist who wishes to survive will continue to try to put poetry into his prose, he will try to get a rhythm and a cadence to his sentences, will try to seek out the colored image, will continue to run after the rare epithet." This effort, he went on to say, will be part of a greater effort to enlarge the scope of French vocabulary, one of the smallest of the major languages.

How may we judge these claims a century later? As for the stylistic contribution of the Goncourts, it seems to have had no major influence on the development of the French language. Scholars have studied the lexical innovations that appear in the *Journal* and have showed the many neologisms and archaisms of their style. But in general these innovations have not lasted. French has changed under the impact, not of the Goncourts, but of modern social upheaval, technological revolution, and widespread incorporation of English words partly in the realm of sports and partly through youth culture. As for the "impressionistic style" that they developed to such an extent, we can say that while its excesses are only too visible, the technique did draw attention to the possibility of giving the language greater flexibility—such as using a noun for an adjective. Concerning the matter of Japanese art, it is certainly true that the Goncourts participated in the introduction of this vogue which at one moment was so great that Zola, looking slightly ridiculous, sat for his portrait in a Japanese robe with Japanese bibelots around. But Japanese art was little more than an extended fad, and if the Goncourts' only claim to immortality resided in the introduction of the East to French culture, they would already be forgotten. Even their rehabilitation of eighteenth-century French art, something they thought was unquestioned and unquestionable, has come under scrutiny. But while scholars have shown that the previous century had not been as neglected as the Goncourts claimed,[5] they did play a role in its revival, and their *L'Art du dix-huitième siècle* is still used today by students of art history, a fact which suggests the importance and solidity of their work in this field. We must accord them a modest plus here.

Finally, they say, that as the authors of *Germinie Lacerteux*, they created a prototype for an entirely new kind of literature. Here they are right. This novel led directly to Zola's *L'Assommoir* and through it to a whole generation of fiction dealing with the working class. Their influence was also strongly felt by Joris-Karl Huysmans, since *Les Soeurs Vatard* (1879) of his Naturalistic period owes much to the Goncourts. Their physiological analysis of Germinie, already anticipated in *Soeur Philomène*, constituted a new and valid literary manner of exploring the human organism. Balzac had understood the importance of the milieu; the Goncourts, even more than Zola, contributed to our realization that our character owes much to our physiology.

But contributing to the establishment of an historical "school" does not constitute the only manner in which one may contribute to the literature of a culture. The Goncourts were also trying to reform the novel itself. As we have seen, they considered the word *roman* a synonym for a story that tells a lie, and turning once again to the preface of *Chérie*, we find that Edmond summed up their views on this matter: "Yes, I believe . . . that adventures, the contriving of bookish episodes, have been fully exploited by Soulié, Sue, by the great creators of imaginative fiction of the beginning of the century, and my thought is that the last step in the evolution of the novel . . . is to do a book of pure analysis: a book for which—I have tried and failed—a young man will find perhaps a new label." This attitude was no late development of the Goncourts. Their *Journal* frequently spoke of the misery of having to create a plot. One quotation by Edmond is particularly revealing:

What a misfortune not to have had the opportunity to write our revolutionary catechism of art. How amusing it would have been, concerning Raphaël, concerning some widely admired painting, to show how little the restorers have left of the original paint, even of the original design of the master. . . .Then concerning a bit of Henry II pottery, to show how imperfect the clay is, how pitiful is its ornamentation, and yet how insanely high the prices are. And in this way to tell it all, for three hundred pages, stamping, overturning established positions, age-old favorites, the syllabi of the professors of aesthetics, of the Institute, all that old artistic faith, more stubborn and yet more lacking in criteria than religious faith.[6]

What the Goncourts really wanted to write, judging from this passage, was not a traditional story but a vast satire debunking all personal, artistic, and social sacred cows, to show the hypocrisy of their culture in its institutions and its values. Their friend Gustave Flaubert actually wrote a little-known work somewhat in this tradition under the title of *Bouvard et Pécuchet* (published 1881), an example of the type of writing that we called in Chapter 1 an "Anatomy." Centuries earlier Rabelais had done something of the sort in his monumental work, although he built his dissection of the world and its mores around the thread of a plot. That the anatomy was a form natural to the Goncourts is visible in their first work of fiction, *En 18 . .* as well as in the myriad essays and disgressions that appear in later novels. But the two brothers discovered that the public did not respond to plotless literature; it wanted the eternal patterns of romance. Had the Goncourts truly believed in writing what they wanted and had not tried to cater to public taste, they might have been recognized in the twentieth century as the anatomists of their age. But whether it was the powerful influence of the standard traditions of the novel, or whether it was their own vanity that wanted their books to sell, the Goncourts always felt obliged to create some plot, protesting against this necessity every step of the way. As a consequence, their novels sometimes seem to be caught halfway between two genres, failing to succeed completely in either. The plots are defective, and the analyses stop short of that total commitment and exuberance which marked the brilliance of Rabelais. *Charles Demailly*, *Madame Gervaisais*, and *Chérie* suffer the most from this indecisiveness, and we may call them solid failures, whose only value today is as documents that shed light on social customs of the day and on the artistic development of Jules and Edmond. The other works of fiction, despite some weaknesses, deserve a better reputation. *Renée Mauperin*, *Manette Salomon*, and *La Faustin* all have their defects but are not as inadequate as has often been claimed by critics judging them according to standards of fiction created by Balzac. We have tried to show that in fact the Goncourts were trying to create a new type of fiction, not one in which the milieu supports and enriches the plot, but one in which the plot is broken up and fragmented with the results that both plot and milieu are subordinated to a basic theme.

This theme, as we have shown in the preceding chapters, was first presented by the Goncourts themselves in *En 18 . .* as being pessimistic determinism, but a study of their fiction shows that it is far better described as the struggle between illusion and reality. In making this theme central to their fiction, the Goncourts were hardly original, for the theme is as old as literature itself. But one can say that it is unusual in nineteenth-century fiction to have everything organized around it. To generalize to the point of danger, after the destruction of the *ancien régime* with the French Revolution, after a brief period of nostalgia for the good old days, writers began to look forward in an effort to find some new ideals. On the personal level, Romantic poets set out on a quest for the ideal woman and perfect love; others sought new religious ideals; the Parnassians and Flaubert strove to arrive at perfection in Art; and on the wider social level, most thinkers looked forward to the day when mankind would arrive at a better, even a perfect society. Liberal humanitarianism and Marxism are typical nineteenth-century beliefs. Even if the explorer was uncertain of his goal, he desired as did Baudelaire in "Le Voyage" to plunge into the unknown and find "something new." This quest for perfection was progressively revealed as a goal impossible to attain, as indicated by the pessimism of the later years of the century. Yet, while Rimbaud in "Le Bateau ivre" ("The Drunken Boat") tells in 1871 of the failure of the quest for the ideal, his narrative poem is built around a linear plot, the quest.

The Goncourts never had any belief in Progress, and hence had no disillusionment concerning the quest for the ideal. They had no illusions about the possibility of any viable restored monarchy; they despised the bourgeoisie and the working class; and they felt that no matter what the social structures might be, mankind never progressed at all. (Did not Edmond write a farce entitled *Down with Progress*?) They saw society as essentially static, capable only of creating the illusion of improvement. As critics of their times they were eager to show the sham behind the pretensions to glory and virtue, both of the Second Empire (1852-70) and of the Republic after the fall of Napoleon III. But the illusions of society were not their only concern. They dealt with the same problem on the individual level, believing that the only "progress" was through time on the road to death. In showing the illusions of human desire, they used varied and at times imaginative techniques. Descriptions of nature, dialogue, diaries, and direct essays all play their role. But perhaps the most striking device is the use of the theater, the mask, pantomime, which in one form or another is found in all their fiction. Their initial use of the mask of illusion covering reality was traditional, as we have shown in *En 18 . .* and *Charles Demailly*. But then they began to realize that human life was more complicated, that illusions could influence reality or even become reality. Sometimes all these ways of looking at the human condition are to be found juxtaposed in the same novel. When the Goncourts got to the point of making the characters—and even the reader— doubt the nature of reality itself, they anticipated some of the literary preoccupations of the twentieth century and, because of this timeliness, should be better known. Certainly, their three finest creations—*Germinie Lacerteux*, *La Fille Elisa*, and *Les Frères Zemganno*—owe much of their value to the Goncourts' concern with these matters.

That they are *not* better known is due not not only to the arrogance of these two brothers, or to some genuine weakness in their fiction, but also to the fact that the Goncourts were perhaps too much ahead of their time. It was not until the disasters of the twentieth century had descended upon the Western world that Europeans and even Americans faced up to the emptiness of the nineteenth-century concept of progress. Modern writers like Pirandello, Beckett, Ionesco, and Genêt are forever dealing with the themes of illusion and reality. It is significant, incidentally, that these writers are playwrights. The stage, an arena of illusion in itself, is an excellent place to discuss these problems. Although not influenced by the Goncourts, whose power to shape future generations of writers had faded out, their work has continued and developed many of these techniques. If we reread the Goncourts with the realization of the centrality of this theme in their work, their novels will appear in a more favorable light.

In addition to dealing imaginatively with reality, in addition to leaving the *Journal* as a document of their age and to making modest contributions to the language and to the history of art, in addition to writing three very superior novels, they opened the realm of fiction to the working class. Because of these real successes, the Goncourts seem destined to have an enduring and respectable place in the history of French literature.

One final comment is in order. Other writers of that day also turned their attention to the sufferings of the working classes, but they often let their sympathy for these victims of social exploitation lead them into idealizing them simply *because* they were victims. One thinks, for instance, of Victor Hugo's *Les Misérables*, and of a character like Fantine. The Goncourts scoffed at such sentimental idealism, preferring to paint a more human picture. They showed in *Germinie Lacerteux* and in *La Fille Elisa* the lower classes as true victims of social injustice but never assumed that victims were inherently virtuous. Zola, who had learned so much from the Goncourts, understood this fact and kept it in mind when writing his great masterpiece, *Germinal*, although later in his life he let his vision become less realistic and more sentimental. Inevitably, this balanced position of the Goncourts was attacked from both sides. The political Right did not wish to admit that there was misery and exploitation; the Left was reluctant to accept the fact that workers could be evil. If the keen ability, such as that possessed by the Goncourts, to see beyond a simplistic moral façade to the more baffling ethical and ontological complexities of human nature had been more widespread, the twentieth century might have avoided some of the deadly struggles caused by an oversimplified vision of man and ethics. Through their work, the Goncourts repudiated impossible dreams of perfection and also the complacent bourgeois illusions which claim that all is basically well. While their penetrating insight made them so pessimistic that they were incapable of action and reduced them to the role of eternal spectators, they should not be scorned. Mankind will always need to be reminded of the limits of human achievement.

Notes and References

Chapter One

1. All references to the *Journal des Goncourt: Mémoires de la vie littéraire* are taken from the edition of Robert Ricatte, published in Monaco by Les Editions de L'Imprimerie Nationale de Monaco in 22 vols. (1956-59). This integral edition supersedes the incomplete 1935-36 edition published under the auspices of the Académie Goncourt, and the edition published during Edmond's lifetime. The numbers in parenthesis in references to this work and to all works are, unless otherwise indicated, page references. Vol. 18, p. 151; March 18, 1892.

2. Alidor Delzant, *Les Goncourt* (Paris: Charpentier, 1889), pp. 5-7. Delzant was a friend of Edmond, and the biography was overseen and approved by him.

3. André Billy, *Les Frères Goncourt* (Paris: Flammarion, 1954), trans. as *The Goncourt Brothers* by Margaret Shaw (New York: Horizon, 1960), p. 21. This work is the best general biography of the Goncourts available in English.

4. Cited by Delzant, *op. cit.*, pp. 18-19, from *La Maison d'un Artiste* of Edmond de Goncourt, Vol. 1, p. 355. Unless otherwise indicated, all references to the Goncourts' work are taken from the "Edition définitive" published under the auspices of the Académie Goncourt.

5. Letter of September 29, 1849; cited from *Lettres de Jules de Goncourt*, p. 56.

6. *Journal*, Vol. 21, p. 136 (November 29, 1895).

7. Cited from Billy, *op. cit.*, pp. 26-27.

8. Vol. 4, p. 40 (June 26, 1860).

9. Vol. 5, p. 106.

10. Cited by François Fosca, *Edmond et Jules de Goncourt* (Paris: A. Michel, 1941), p. 33.

11. *Ibid.*, p. 35.

12. *Op. cit.*, p. 28.

13. Fosca, p. 43.

14. Robert Ricatte, *La Création romanesque chez les Goncourt*, I, 1851-70 (Paris: Colin, 1953). This massive French doctoral thesis is the principal scholarly study to date of the Goncourts' fiction. It is a mine of information and makes penetrating critical judgments about their work (up to 1870). Indispensable.

15. *Ibid.*, p. 70.

16. *Op. cit.*, p. 49.

17. *Anatomy of Criticism: Four Essays*, (Princeton, N.J.: Princeton University Press, 1957).

18. *Ibid.*, p. 310. Frye adds wryly that if there is an appearance of care-lessness, it results only from the carelessness of the reader or his tendency to judge by a novel-centered conception of fiction.

19. *Ibid.*, p. 309.

20. Delzant, p. 316.

21. *Op. cit.*, p. 56.

22. Delzant, p. 316.

23. Later reprinted under the definitive title: *Quelques Créatures de ce temps*.

24. *L'Art du XVIIIe siècle*, Vol. 1, p. 95.

25. *Ibid.*, pp. 9-10.

26. *Préfaces et manifestes littéraires*, 187-188.

27. See Louis L. Curcio, *The Goncourts Historians* (Rosario, Argentina, 1951) and Seymour S. Simches, *Le Romantisme et le goût esthétique du XVIIIe siècle* (Paris: Presses Universitaires de France, 1964).

28. Curcio, p. 30. In 1854, the Goncourts had published a brief pam-phlet entitled *La Révolution dans les moeurs* in which they made clear that they preferred the *ancien régime* to modern times. See Billy, p. 52.

29. Billy, p. 56.

30. Published later by Edmond with three separate titles: *La DuBarry* (1878), *Madame de Pompadour* (1878), *La Duchesse de Châteauroux* (1879).

31. *Préfaces et manifestes littéraires*, pp. 184-85. See Curcio, p. 72.

32. *Journal*, Vol. 11, p. 188 (April 6, 1878).

33. *Ibid.*, Vol. 7, p. 86 (May 22, 1865); and Vol. 11, p. 199 (July 22, 1878). In the latter entry he explains that historiography takes all one's time and does not basically absorb one, or get one outside one's self.

34. Cited by Delzant, p. 310.

35. *Journal*, Vol. 1, p. 29. See also Preface to 1887 edition of the *Journal*.

36. E.g., *Pages from the Goncourt Journal*, ed., trans., and introduced by Robert Baldick (London and New York: Oxford, 1962) and *Paris under Siege, 1870-1871: From the Goncourt Journal*, ed. and trans. George Becker (Ithaca: Cornell University Press, 1969).

37. *Journal*, Vol. 7, p. 15 (October 24, 1864).

38. *Ibid.*, Vol. 4, p. 152 (January 14, 1861).

39. *Ibid.*, Vol. 5, p. 26 (November 24, 1861).

Chapter Two

1. *Journal*, Vol. 21, p. 154 (December 26, 1895).

2. *Journal des Débats*, Jan. 30, 1860; cited by Delzant, *op. cit.*, p. 70.

3. Fosca, *op. cit.*, pp. 172-73.

4. Billy, *op. cit.*, p. 78.

5. *Journal*, Vol. 2, p. 163 (October, 1857).

6. *Ibid.*, Vol. 3, p. 22 (August, 1858).

7. One can imagine Uchard's horror at their use of his indiscretion. See Ricatte, *op. cit.*, p. 142, and *Journal*, Vol. 3, p. 212 (January 28, 1860).

8. Ricatte, p. 147.

9. *Journal*, Vol. 13, p. 14 (February 20, 1883).

10. *Ibid.*, Vol. 14, p. 133 (June 18, 1886).

11. *Ibid.*, Vol. 14, p. 152 (October 11, 1886).

12. *Ibid.*, Vol. 4, p. 118 (November 29, 1860).

13. *Ibid.*, Vol. 5, p. 137 (July 13, 1862).

14. *Ibid.*, Vol. 7, p. 161 (February 1, 1866).

15. *Ibid.*, Vol. 16, p. 58 (April 8, 1889).

16. *Ibid.*, Vol. 2, p. 155 (August 20-26, 1857).

17. *Ibid.*, Vol. 4, p. 248 (October 1, 1861).

18. *Ibid.*, Vol. 3, p. 116 (May, 1859); Vol. 4, p. 96 (October 3, 1860).

19. *Ibid.*, Vol. 6, p. 200 (May 1, 1864).

20. *Ibid.*, Vol. 7, p. 100 (July 23, 1865).

21. The medical symptoms are not entirely convincing despite various studies that have claimed that they were. See Ricatte, pp. 144-47.

22. For the details of this incident, see Ricatte, p. 154.

23. Billy, p. 107.

24. *Journal*, Vol. 4, pp. 152-53 and 161 (January 14 and March 2, 1861).

25. Fosca, p. 180.

26. *Journal*, Vol. 2, p. 151 (August 5, 1857).

27. *Ibid.*, Vol. 3, p. 131 (June 12, 1859).

28. *Ibid.*, Vol. 5, p. 141 (July 28, 1862).

29. *Ibid.*, Vol. 5, p. 173 (December 28, 1862).

30. *Ibid.*, Vol. 8, p. 80 (January 24, 1865).

31. *Ibid.*, Vol. 8, p. 245 (June 18, 1870).

32. Ricatte, p. 171.

33. *Ibid.*, p. 184. See also G. Flaubert, *Correspondance* (Paris: Conard, 1910), 3e serie, p. 282, letter of July 1861 to E. and J. de Goncourt.

34. Ricatte, p. 175.

35. *Ibid.*, p. 190.

36. In "Edmond et Jules de Goncourt," *Les Contemporains*, 3e série. (Paris: Lecène, Oudin, 1895).

37. Cambridge, England: Cambridge University Press, 1957.

38. *Histoire de la littérature française* (Paris: Fayard, 1967), Vol. 2, p. 531. Joris-Karl Huysmans, on the other hand, shows in his novel *A Rebours* (1884) a decadent hero, Des Esseintes, who likes their style precisely because it acts as an irritant to a jaded sensibility.

Chapter Three

1. This idea dates from March-April, 1855. See Ricatte, p. 191.

2. *Charles Demailly*, pp. 96-97.

3. *Journal*, January 24, 1859 and March 11, 1859, as cited by Ricatte, p. 213.

4. Vol. 2, p. 162 (October 1857).

5. Ricatte, p. 238.

6. *Journal*, Vol. 5, p. 146 (August 16, 1862).

7. *Ibid.*, Vol. 5, p. 143 (August 2, 1862). This episode they transferred to fiction by including cupping in the treatment of Renée.

8. *Ibid.*, Vol. 5, pp. 155-57 (August 21, 1862).

9. *Ibid.*, Vol. 10, p. 45 (December 3, 1871); cited by E. Auerbach, *Mimesis: The Representation of Reality in Western Literature* (New York: Doubleday Anchor, 1953), p. 439.

10. *Journal*, Vol. 5, p. 229 (December 14, 1862).

11. *Ibid.*, Vol. 7, p. 195 (August 30, 1866).

12. *Ibid.*, Vol. 7, p. 201 (September 10, 1866).

13. Vol. 3, p. 174 (December 7, 1859).

14. *Les Romanciers naturalistes* in *Oeuvres complètes d'Emile Zola*, ed. M. Le Blond (Paris: Bernouard, 1928), Vol. 44, p. 201.

15. Mlle de Varandeuil is based on a real-life character, their own aunt, Mlle Cornélie de Courmont.

16. See Ricatte, pp. 277-78 for details.

17. *Journal*, Vol. 7, p. 63 (March, 1865).

18. *Ibid.*, Vol. 7, p. 100 (July 23, 1865).

19. Cited by Billy, p. 138.

Chapter Four

1. *Journal*, Vol. 21, p. 135 (November 28, 1895).

2. *Ibid.*, Vol. 18, p. 122 (January 30, 1892).

3. *Ibid.*, Vol. 4, p. 99 (October 12, 1860). The use of the first-person form was a convention of the Goncourts, but it meant "we" until Jules's death.

4. *Ibid.*, Vol. 4, p. 151 (January 10, 1861).

5. *Ibid.*, Vol. 5, p. 47 (January, 1862).

6. *Ibid.*, Vol. 4, p. 125 (December 10, 1860).

7. The episode is based on the actual death of Beaurepaire on September 2, 1792.

8. As the play was not produced until 1875, it seemed as if Edmond had imitated Hugo's character Cimourdin in *Quatrevingt-Treize*, but the true chronology makes this impossible.

9. *Journal*, Vol. 15, p. 206 (December 19, 1888).

10. *Ibid.*, Vol. 15, p. 214 (December 25, 1888).

11. *Ibid.*, Vol. 15, pp. 211-13 (December 25, 1888).

12. Vol. 15, p. 221.

Chapter Five

1. See Gustave Geoffroy's essay in the postface to the Edition définitive, p. 355. The Goncourts thought so highly of their friend that their last effort at mutual creation was to write his biography in 1869.

2. Ricatte, p. 306; Vol. 7, p. 191 (August 5, 1866).

3. The quotation is from *Manette Salomon* itself, p. 374, but although applying ostensibly to the hero, Coriolis, it fits the Goncourts perfectly.

4. *Journal*, Vol. 6, p. 208 (May 28, 1864).

5. Charles Baudelaire, *Salon de 1845*, p. 24; cited by Ricatte, p. 359.

6. Ricatte, p. 360.

7. Closely modeled after a Bohemian acquaintance of the Goncourts named Pouthier.

8. *Journal*, Vol. 7, p. 32 (December 12, 1864).

9. Modeled in part on the painter-critic Paul Chenavard, a constant talker on art at Parisian cafés, although his ideas were not always those of the Goncourts. See Ricatte, p. 337; and Joseph Sloane, *Paul Marie Joseph Chenavard, artist of 1848* (Chapel Hill, N.C.: University of North Carolina Press, 1962).

10. *Journal*, Vol. 2, p. 218 (April 13, 1858).

11. Pierre Sabatier, *L'Esthétique des Goncourt* (Paris: Hachette, 1920), pp. 190-91.

12. Vol. 3, p. 105 (February 17, 1859).

13. Another influence may be Charles-Emile Jacque (1813-94). See Ricatte, p. 340.

14. *Journal*, Vol. 8, p. 112 (May 25, 1868).

15. *Ibid.*, p. 113.

16. *Ibid.*, Vol. 8, p. 113 (May 27, 1868).

17. *Ibid.*, Vol. 8, p. 113 (May 30, 1868).

18. *Ibid.*, Vol. 8, p. 140 (September 17, 1868).

19. *Ibid.*, Vol. 8, p. 141 (September 1868).

20. *Ibid.*, Vol. 2, p. 28 (September 17, 1856).

21. On deposit with the Département des Dessins of the Musée du Louvre; Max Fuchs studied it in "Les Goncourt en Italie d'après leurs notes de voyage inédites," in *La Grande Revue*, 1920, Vol. 103, pp. 84-99. The notebook includes some unpublished material.

22. Billy, p. 159, and *Journal*, Vol. 8, pp. 16-17 (April 25, 1867).

23. Cited by Delzant, p. 155.

24. *Journal*, Vol. 8, pp. 109-10 (May 16, 1868).

25. *Ibid.*, Vol. 6, p. 64 (May 5, 1863). This character is a direct transposi-

tion of the Russian Madame Swetchine.

26. This seemingly over-dramatic end reflects in fact the events of their aunt's death. She died while dressing to go to the Papal audience.

27. *Ibid.*, Vol. 8, p. 157 (December 24, 1868).

28. *Ibid.*, Vol. 8, pp. 167-68 (January 31, 1869).

29. *Ibid.*, Vol. 8, p. 188 (March 30, 1869).

30. *Ibid.*, Vol. 8, p. 207 (June 10, 1869).

Chapter Six

1. Noted by Delzant, *op. cit.*, p. 210.

2. This notebook was first in the possession of Alidor Delzant and now is in the René Gimpel collection. See Robert Ricatte, *La Genèse de La Fille Elisa* (Paris: Presses Univ. de France, 1960), pp. 1-21. The text is reproduced on pp. 167-215.

3. Ricatte, *Genèse*, p. 27.

4. *Journal*, Vol. 5, p. 190 (October 29, 1862).

5. *Ibid.*, Vol. 11, p. 119 (December 30, 1876): "I had planned to go a bit further, to put into the manuscript a lot of little discoveries that I could have made concerning the world of prostitution and prisons, but it would perhaps be too much, and also . . . I haven't the courage to work any more on a book that may be banned."

6. Vol. 5, p. 55 (February 16, 1862).

7. Sabatier, *op. cit.*, p. 196, taken from *Idées et sensations*, p. 79.

8. *Op. cit.*, p. 300.

9. Vol. 11, p. 137 (April 4, 1877).

10. *Correspondance*, ed. Conard, 8e série, 1930, p. 25. Letter of April 2, 1877.

Chapter Seven

1. Vol. 11, p. 118.

2. Vol. 11, p. 200 (July 29, 1878).

3. Vol. 11, p. 222.

4. Vol. 11, p. 231 (December 10, 1878). The name Zemganno, which Edmond found in the *Mémoires secrets* of Bachaumont, apparently appealed to him more than the stage name Bendigo, but he never explained why.

5. Vol. 3, p. 171.

6. Vol. 1, p. 165 (March, 1855).

7. Vol. 8, p. 55.

8. Vol. 14, p. 195 (February 6, 1887).

9. Vol. 18, p. 107 (December 17, 1891).

10. Vol. 20, pp. 51-52 (May 3, 1894).

11. See also passages on pp. 228, 233.

12. Vol. 4, p. 231 (September 3, 1861).

13. Vol. 7, p. 45 (January 26, 1865).

14. Miss Tompkins is credible only on the symbolic level. Instead of showing us the growth of her desire for Nello, Edmond treats us to a preposterous scene in which she, like Huysmans' Des Esseintes, smokes in darkness, wallowing on a pile of cushions, while two horses, Erebus and Snowball, cavort around a ring spread with Oriental rugs, while smoking pots of incense give off exotic perfumes (pp. 188-90).

15. *Histoire de la littérature française* (Paris: Fayard, 1967), Vol. 2, p. 530.

Chapter Eight

1. Vol. 5, p. 132.

2. *Ibid.*, Vol. 3, p. 153 (October 12, 1859).

3. *Ibid.*, Vol. 3, p. 169 (November 21, 1859).

4. Vol. 3, p. 173 (December 3, 1859).

5. *Ibid.*, Vol. 4, pp. 159, 171 (February 4 and March 28, 1861).

6. Vol. 11, p. 155.

7. Vol. 12, p. 151n.

8. Vol. 12, p. 110 (April 6, 1881).

9. Inspired by a thirty-year-old memory; see *Journal*, Vol. 12, p. 133 (October 28, 1881).

10. In the *Gil Blas*, February 7, 1882; see *Journal*, Vol. 12, p. 150.

11. Vol. 12, p. 150 (February 7, 1882).

12. *Ibid.*, Vol. 7, p. 96 (July 7).

13. *Ibid.*, Vol. 11, p. 218 (September 30).

14. *Ibid.*, Vol. 13, p. 16 (March 4, 1883).

15. Cited by André Billy, *op. cit.*, p. 234.

16. *Ibid.*, p. 296.

17. *Ibid.*, p. 298.

Chapter Nine

1. *Journal*, Vol. 6, p. 214 (June 16, 1864).

2. *Mimesis*, p. 438.

3. *Littérature et sensation* (Paris: Editions du seuil, 1954), p. 269.

4. Page xi of the Édition définitive.

5. See Seymour Simches, *Le Romantisme et le goût esthétique du XVIIIe siècle* (Paris, P.U.F., 1964).

6. *Journal*, Vol. 12, pp. 24-25 (May 28, 1879).

Selected Bibliography

PRIMARY SOURCES

The principal edition of the Goncourts' work is the "Edition définitive," published under the direction of the Académie Goncourt. It includes the novels, the earlier version (incomplete) of the *Journal*, a volume of theater, Jules's correspondence, and the Goncourts' principal works of history, biography, and art criticism. These volumes do not have any extensive scholarly apparatus, but there is an essay on the work written by a member of the Académie Goncourt included at the end of each work. Published by Flammarion-Fasquelle between the years 1921 and 1936, these volumes are no longer in print. For the year of first publication, see the Chronology at the beginning of this study. As far as works that are in print as of this writing, the *Journal* is now available in its entirety, thanks to the efforts of Robert Ricatte: *Journal; mémoires de la vie littéraire*, texte intégral établi et annoté par Robert Ricatte. Monaco, Imprimerie Nationale, 1956-59, in 22 volumes. Recently *La Fille Elisa* has been republished (Beckers: Antwerp, 1968) and *Germinie Lacerteux*, ed. by E. Caramaschi (Paris: Nizet, 1968).

Translations

The majority of the novels have been translated into English, but many were done prior to World War I and are now so rare as to be virtually unobtainable except in such major research libraries as the Library of Congress and the British Museum. We give below those works of the Goncourts translated recently enough so that there is some hope of obtaining them.

L'Art du XVIIIe siècle
> *French XVIIIth Century Painters*. Tr. R. Ironside. New York: Phaidon, 1948.

La Fille Elisa
> *Elisa, the Story of a Prostitute*. Tr. M. Crosland. London: N. Spearman, and New York: Hillman, 1959.
> *Woman of Paris*. Tr. C. Harrald. London: Elek, 1959.

Les Frères Zemganno
> *The Zemganno Brothers*. Tr. Clark and Allam. London: Redman, 1957.

Germinie Lacerteux
> *Germinie*. Tr. J. Griffith. New York: Grove; and London: Weidenfeld and Nicolson, 1955.

Journal; mémoires de la vie littéraire
> *The Goncourt Journals (1851-1870)*. Edited and translated from the *Journal* of Edmond and Jules de Goncourt, with an introduction and notes and a biographical repertory by Louis Galantière. Garden City, N.Y.: Doubleday, 1958.
> *Pages from the Goncourt Journal*. Edited, translated and introduced by Robert Baldick. London and New York: Oxford University Press, 1962.
> *Paris under Siege, 1870-1871: From the Goncourt Journal*. Edited and translated by George J. Becker, with a historical introduction by Paul H. Beik. Ithaca and London: Cornell University Press, 1969.

SECONDARY SOURCES

AUERBACH, ERICH. *Mimesis: The Representation of Reality in Western Literature.* Trans. from the German by Willard Trask. Garden City, N.Y.: Doubleday Anchor Books, 1953. Original edition, 1946. Compares the Goncourts to Zola, to the latter's advantage.

BALDICK, ROBERT. *The Goncourts.* New York: Hillary House, 1960. A very brief, but excellent summary.

BILLY, ANDRÉ. *The Goncourt Brothers.* Trans. from the French by Margaret Shaw. New York: Horizon, 1960. Original edition, 1954. The best standard biography and available in English.

BOURGET, PAUL. "Edmond et Jules de Goncourt," in *Essais de psychologie contemporaine.* Paris: Plon, 1899. Excellent criticism which has not dated.

CURCIO, LOUIS L. *The Goncourts, Historians.* Rosario, Argentina: Tallerea Gráficos Sudilevsky y Calderon, 1951. This slim volume attempts to fix the limits of the Goncourts' ability as historians.

DELZANT, ALIDOR. *Les Goncourt.* Paris: Charpentier, 1889. This biography is of special value because it was overseen and approved by Edmond.

FOSCA, FRANÇOIS. *Edmond et Jules de Goncourt.* Paris: Albin Michel, 1941. An excellent general study.

FRYE, NORTHROP. *Anatomy of Criticism.* Princeton, N.J.: Princeton University Press, 1957. A brilliant treatise on literary criticism.

LEMAÎTRE, JULES. "Edmond et Jules de Goncourt," in *Les Contemporains*, 3e serie. Paris: Lecène, Oudin, 1895. Good commentary on the Goncourts' style.

RICATTE, ROBERT. *La Création romanesque chez les Goncourt (1851-1870).* Paris: Colin, 1953. Indispensable. The leading critical study of the Goncourts up to the time of Jules's death.

——*La Genèse de La Fille Elisa.* Paris: Presses Universitaries de France, 1960. Good scholarly study.

RICHARD, JEAN-PIERRE. "Deux écrivains épidermiques: Edmond et Jules de Goncourt," in *Littérature et sensation.* Paris: Editions de seuil, 1954. Biased and hostile to the Goncourts, but often very perceptive.

SABATIER, PIERRE. *L'Esthétique des Goncourt.* Paris: Hachette, 1920. An older study, but still valuable.

SIMCHES, SEYMOUR. *Le Romantisme et le gout esthétique du XVIIIe siècle* Paris: Presses Universities de France, 1964. This study tries to show that the eighteenth century was not rediscovered by the Goncourts. It was already well known.

ULLMANN, STEPHEN. *Style in the French Novel.* Cambridge, England: Cambridge University Press, 1957. Contains a chapter on the Goncourts.

ZOLA, EMILE. "Edmond et Jules de Goncourt," in *Les Romanciers naturalistes.* Paris: Charpentier, 1881. Also available in the LeBlond edition of Zola's *Oeuvres complètes*, vol. 44. Paris: Typographie Bernouard, 1928. A favorable study of his colleagues in the Naturalistic novel.

Index

Place names, names of fictional characters, and names of modern scholars are not included. In listing periodicals and titles, definite and indefinite articles have been ignored; *Le Paris*, for example, is listed under P.

A bas le progrès, 131, 148
Abbatucci, Mlle M., 136-37
Abou Hassan, 18
Académie Goncourt, 5, 139-40, 143, 151
Les Actrices, 131
Antoine, A., 82
Arnould, S., 28
L'Art du dix-huitième siècle, 26, 145
L'Artiste, 24-25
Aurevilly, B. d', 35, 98, 101, 135, 139
Bachaumont, L. Petit de, 156
Balzac, H. de, 13, 19-20, 30, 34, 36, 43, 45, 55, 57, 65, 73, 93, 118, 147
Banville, Th. de, 25, 35, 139
Baudillart, H., 28
Beaurepaire, N.-J. de, 154
Beckett, S., 79, 149
Bernhardt, S., 132
Le Bien Public, 139
Blamont, 18
Blanc, L., 16
Bonnetain, P., 141
Boucher, 26
Bouilhet, L., 44
Brohan, M., 35-36, 39
Brunetière, F., 135
Byron, 22

Camus, A., 16
Carron, Father, 57
Champfleury, 39, 45, 72
Chardin, 26
Charles Demailly, 33-43, 44, 60, 66, 70, 122, 125, 138, 147, 149
Charpentier, G., 117, 133
Chateaubriand, F. R. de, 103
Chenavard, P., 155
Chennevières, Ph. de, 139
Chérie, 94, 136-39, 144, 147

Cladel, L., 139
Claretie, J., 72
Classicism, 69, 73-74, 132
Colmant, A., 63, 68
Comte, A., 45
Corneille, P., 73, 132
Courbet, G., 87, 90
Courmont, Mlle C. de, 154
Courmont, Nephtalie L. de, 14, 97

Dante, 21
Darwin, Ch., 65
Daudet, A., 5, 30, 73, 98, 102, 117, 133, 139, 141
Daumier, H., 21
David, L., 26, 86
Debucourt, 26
Debureau, 96
Decamps, A., 87, 90-91
Delacroix, E., 87
Dentu, 26, 33
Descaves, L., 141
Doumergue, R., 46
Drolling, M., 86
La DuBarry, 152
La Duchesse de Châteauroux, 152
Dumas, A. *père*, 77
Dumas, A. *fils*, 110
Duranty, E., 45
Duveau, L.-J.-N., 87

L'Eclair, 24-25
En 18. ., 18-24, 34, 36, 39, 41-43, 52-53, 66, 122, 147, 149
Eugénie (Empress ——— de Montijo), 76

La Faustin, 131-36, 147
Félix, D., 132-33
Félix, L., 132-33
La Femme au XVIIIe siècle, 27-28
Le Figaro, 141
La Fille Elisa, 63, 108-18, 144, 149, 150
Flandrin, H., 88
Flaubert, G., 13, 16, 35, 40, 42-45, 53, 72, 73, 76, 117, 118, 139, 147, 148, 153

Fragonard, 26
Les Frères Zemganno, 60, 119-30, 132, 134, 135, 149
Fromentin, E., 13, 139

Gaïffe, A., 34
Le Gaulois, 97
Gautier, Th., 16, 24, 35
Gavarni, 25, 85, 103
Genêt, J., 79, 149
Genettes, Mme R. des, 117
Gerdès, 18
Germinie Lacerteux, 62-72, 95, 97, 98, 109, 110, 118, 119, 131, 132, 144, 146, 149, 150; (*as play*), 82, 83, 85
Gibbon, E., 30
Gide, A., 116
Gil Blas, 140
Goncourt, Jules de, birth, schooling, 13; description, 14; sketches, 15; trip to southern France, Africa, 17; further travels, 18; collaboration in writing 23-24; journalism, 24-25; arrest on obscenity charge, 25; art criticism, 25-27; writing of history, 27-28; writing biographies, 28; begin *Journal*, 29; views on the novel, 31; their style, 52-53; friendship with Gavarni, 85; ill-health, 86, 96; settle in Auteuil, 97; trip to Rome, 98; death 103
Goncourt, Edmond de, birth, schooling, law work, 13; Treasury employee, 14; National Guardsman, 14; description, 14; love of bibelots, 14-15; years in artist's studio, 16; trip to southern France, Africa, 17; further travels, 18; collaboration in writing, 23-24; journalism, 24-25; arrest on obscenity charge, 25; art criticism, 25-27; writing of history, 27-28; writing biographies, 28; begin *Journal*, 29; views on the novel, 31, 144-47; their style, 52-53; lithography, 85; friendship with Gavarni, 85; settle in Auteuil, 97; trip to Rome, 98; experiences with siege of Paris and Commune, 105-8; founding Académie Goncourt, 139-40; le "grenier," 140; the "Manifeste des Cinq," 140; death, 141

Greuze, 26
Guiches, G., 141
La Guimard, 131
Guizot, F., 59

Hanlon Lees, 129
Hardy, T., 67
Henriette Maréchal, 75-79, 85, 86, 97, 122
Hervilly, E. d', 149
L'Histoire de la société française pendant la Révolution, 27
L'Histoire de la société française pendant le Directoire, 28
Hokusaï, 141
Les Hommes de lettres (*see Charles Demailly*)
Hugo, V., 65, 74, 76, 101, 110, 136, 143, 150, 154
Huot de Goncourt, A., 13
Huot de Goncourt, Marc-Pierre, 13, 14
Huot de Goncourt, Mme Marc-Pierre, 13, 14
Huysmans, J.-K., 64, 128, 146, 153, 157

Idées et sensations, 85, 145
Ingres, D., 59, 87
Ionesco, E., 149

Janin, J., 19, 34
Journal, 29-31, 85
Jouvin, B., 61

Kock, P. de, 41

Labille, A., 58
La Lorette, 63
Loti, P., 5

Madame de Pompadour, 152
Madame Gervaisais, 97-102, 108, 118, 147
Mademoiselle Clairon, 13
Mademoiselle de Rochedragon (*see La Patrie en danger*)
La Maison d'un artiste, 14
Les Maîtresses de Louis XV, 28, 29
Malingre, R., 46, 62, 63, 68, 108
Manette Salomon, 85-97, 122, 145, 147
Margueritte, P., 122, 125, 141
Maria, 62, 109
Marie-Antoinette (Queen), 28, 80

83586

Marx, K., 148
Mathilde (Princess ―――― Bonaparte), 72, 75, 76, 102, 117, 136
Maupassant, Guy de, 34, 91
Millet, J.-F., 87, 95
Molière, 73
Monselet, Ch., 34
Morgantini, L., 129
Murger, H., 25, 35
Musset, A. de, 73
Les Mystères des Théatres, 25

Nadar, 25, 34

Le Nain jaune, 98
Napoleon III, 106, 148
Naturalism, 5, 45, 52, 67-69, 120, 135, 141
La Nuit de Saint-Sylvestre, 18, 25

Le Paris, 24, 25
Passy, B., 56, 61
Passy, L., 22, 56
La Patrie en danger, 79-83
Perugino, 87
Pirandello, L., 79, 126, 149
Portraits intimes du XVIIIe siècle, 28
Pouthier, 155
La Presse, 61
Proust, M., 53
Prud'hon, 26

Quelques créatures de ce temps, 25, 152

Rabelais, F., 147
Rachel (Eliz.-Rachel Félix), 132
Racine, J., 73, 132, 133
Raphael, 87
Le Réalisme, 45
Realism, 45, 69, 72, 74, 75, 87, 106, 120, 140
Renan, E., 65, 106
Renée Mauperin, 55-62, 86, 118, 122, 147
La Révolution dans les moeurs, 152
Rimbaud, A., 148
Rolland, R., 82
Romanticism, 17, 19, 22, 69, 74, 87
Rosny, *l'aîné*, 141
Rousseau, Th., 87, 95

Shakespeare, 122
Les Saint-Aubin, 26
Saint-Victor, P. de, 35, 139
Sainte-Beuve, Ch. A. de, 25, 45, 102
Le Salon de 1852, 25
Sand, G., 34
Sans Titre, 18
Sarcey, F., 82
Sartre, J.-P., 16
Scholl, A., 34
Soeur Philomène, 44-52, 53, 55, 65-67, 70, 98, 100, 111, 134
Soulié, F., 146
Stendhal, 5, 13, 73, 98
Sterne, L., 23
Sue, E., 146
Swetchine, Mme, 156

Tahureau, J., 25
Taine, H., 45, 65
Le Temps, 82, 86
La Tour, 26
Tournemine, Ch. de, 87, 91
Toynbee, A., 30

Uchard, M., 35, 36, 39, 153
Utamaro, 141

Valentin, H., 34
Vallès, J., 135
Velpeau, A.-M., 45
Venet, 34
Veuillot, L., 139
Villedeuil, Ch. de, 24
Les Vignettistes Gravelot, Cochin-Eisen, Moreau, 26
Vigny, A. de, 78
Villemessant, A. de, 34, 61
Une Voiture de masques (see *Quelques créatures de ce temps*)
Voltaire, 43

Watteau, A., 26
Watteau, 26, 41
Worth, 137

Zeller, P., 137
Ziem, F., 87, 91
Zola, E., 13, 37, 55, 65, 68, 72, 73, 97, 110, 112, 117-19, 133, 135, 137, 139-41, 145, 150

DATE DUE

GAYLORD			PRINTED IN U.S.A